GOOD THINGS FOR ORGANIZING

GOOD THINGS WITH MARTHA STEWART LIVING

GOOD THINGS FOR ORGANIZING

Originally published in book form by Martha Stewart Living
Omnimedia, Inc. in 2001. Published simultaneously by Clarkson
Potter/Publishers, Oxmoor House, Inc., and Leisure Arts.

A portion of this work was previously published in
MARTHA STEWART LIVING.

Printed in the United States of America.

Library of Congress Cataloging-in-Publication Data
Good things for organizing/editors of Martha Stewart Living.
    1. Storage in the home. 2. House cleaning. 1. Martha Stewart Living.
TX309.G66 2001
648'.8 – dc21   00-068805

ISBN   0-8487-1990-5 (hardcover)
           0-8487-1991-3 (paperback)

Executive Editor: Kathleen Hackett
Deputy Editor: Alice Gordon
Associate Art Director: Brooke Hellewell
Assistant Managing Editor: Shelley Berg
Text by Lesley Porcelli
Assistant Editor: Christine Moller
Assistant Art Director: Alanna Jacobs
Copy Editor: Talley Sue Hohlfeld
Senior Design Production Associate: Duane Stapp
Design Production Associate: Laura Grady

90 Labels No. 25   1 3/16 × 3/4

Reyburn's GUMMED LABELS

PART TWO

WORKING

WHAT DO YOU DO TO STAY
ORGANIZED?

PERHAPS THE QUESTION I'M MOST ASKED IS "HOW DO YOU DO IT ALL?" The answer is quite simple. I'm organized. Not fanatically organized like some of my friends, whose shelves of books are neater than those in the Library of Congress, nor like others whose clothes are categorized by color, season, size, and length. But organized enough so that I don't feel disorganized, or sloppy, or frantic, and, when pressed, I know I can put my hands on that photo, or memo, or book, or birth certificate that someone needs that day.

My life is extremely busy. I have more than one home, and really more than one job. I often feel as if I live in my car, traveling from my television studio in Connecticut

to one of my two offices in New York City. I travel a lot both in the United States and overseas. I use mobile phones, regular phones, and e-mail to stay in touch minute-to-minute. I have a handheld organizer and computers that give me instant access to my ever-changing schedules, appointments, to-do lists, and messages. I have programmed the phones, so that instead of memorizing the phone numbers of associates and friends, I only have to memorize one- or two-digit numbers in order to call them. At home I keep only current files and projects I am working on at the time. All other papers, all other files, are neatly organized in the "memory" of my computer or in file cabinets at my Connecticut office.

My house is always being reorganized, and I am constantly devising new ways to order my "stuff": collectibles, cameras, games, pets' toys, and even pantry supplies, so that I can find everything I need and want. Storage of all kinds abounds in my house, from fine, linen-covered boxes labeled with P-touch identification cards for small items like eyeglasses and engraved stationery, to larger, rigid plastic tubs for attic and basement storage.

And of course a great deal of credit must go to my housekeepers and my talented assistants, Julia Eisemann and Annie Armstrong, who are empowered to help with this "organizing." Even if I can't find my glue, my special calligrapher's pen, or my colored Post-its, I can be certain they can.

Martha Stewart

If I have three **THINGS TO DO,**
I do the easiest one first, so I feel I
accomplished something. I do the
hardest thing last, in case it really
bogs me down.

STEPHEN DRUCKER
EDITOR IN CHIEF, EDITORIAL CORE

When I moved into my neighborhood,
I got **BUSINESS CARDS** from
the cleaners, restaurants, delis, liquor
stores, etc., and put them in a Rolodex
in a kitchen drawer by the phone.

WHITNEY JEWETT
ASSOCIATE PRODUCER, INTERNET

I organize my **GROCERY** shopping
list by the layout of the store.

ALISON VANEK
PHOTOGRAPHY ARCHIVE MANAGER

I pay my **BILLS** online.

ROMY POKORNY
HOME/KEEPING EDITOR, INTERNET

Junk mail goes directly in the trash.
I use **CLOTHESPINS** to organize
the rest. Each clothespin is labeled,
one each for unpaid bills, thank you
notes, magazine subscriptions, correspondence, and invitations. I keep
all clothespinned items in a basket.
Once I've taken care of the items,
I fasten the empty clothespin to the
rim of the basket, a reminder that
an item is finished, even though it's
rare those clothespins are empty.

JODI LEVINE
DEPUTY EDITOR, HOLIDAYS/CRAFTS

MANILA FOLDERS—lots of them.

DEBRA PUCHALLA
ASSISTANT MANAGING EDITOR

I grew up ski racing, and there was a lot
of gear to remember. We wrote a "Do
You Have?" **CHECKLIST** on a chalkboard in the mudroom above the door.
My father still uses it.

GEORGIA LIEBMAN
EDITORIAL ASSISTANT

I make a **MASTER LIST** that lists
all the other lists I have to make.

BRIAN HARTER ANDRIOLA
ASSISTANT STYLE EDITOR

I do **15 TO 20 MINUTES** of light
cleaning and organizing every day. My
apartment never gets out of control,
and I can have it really clean in an hour.

JODI NAKATSUKA
DEPUTY PHOTO EDITOR

I use **BINDER CLIPS** to seal opened
packages of food.

SCOT SCHY
ART DIRECTOR

Rather than keeping magazines that
have one or two articles in them that I
want to save, I make **INSPIRATION
BOOKS** for travel, architecture,
cooking, gardening, and decoration.
I tear out the articles I want to keep
and file them in the appropriate folder.

LINDA KOCUR
ART DIRECTOR, MARTHA BY MAIL

PART ONE

LIVING

chapter
one

KITCHEN

IMAGINE THE PERFECT KITCHEN: AN OVERSIZE REFRIGERATOR, AN ENDLESS windowsill of fresh herbs, a cutting block big enough to lie down on, and a Jetsons-style sink that seizes dirty cereal bowls, washes them, and reshelves them. The last still lies ahead, and the rest require a kitchen larger than most. But even a few changes can make any kitchen more user-friendly. Store your cooking utensils by the stove top, and they'll practically fly into your hand. File your recipes on your computer, and retrieve them almost as fast as you think of them. Coax pots and pans to nestle peacefully instead of waging war whenever the cupboard opens. Even if your kitchen is the size of a shower stall, getting organized can give you all the room you need to cook up a grand meal.

DISHES

CUTLERY

POTS & PANS

COUNTERS

PANTRIES

RECIPES

OPEN SHELVES

Exposed shelves are more than a place to put stuff—they're also a showcase when creatively arranged. In the kitchen at Skylands, her house in Maine, Martha created her own great wall of china, opposite, by taking every white dish she could find out of her cupboards and putting it on display. Below the shelves on a porcelain fishmonger's table, left, white containers keep disparate elements neat: Flatware lies on white platters, utensils are stored in various white pitchers, and even onions and garlic await use on white plates. The best part of this setup is that it's also quite practical—dishes are located and reached in an instant.

CHINA CABINETS

Wooden cabinets with window-pane doors allow you to display your china while shielding it from dust. At left, pieces are spaced out generously, a precaution against damage. When you want to hide a cabinet's contents, cover the glass with a curtain that blends with the color of your kitchen or china. Measure a fabric panel to be an inch larger than the glass on all sides when hemmed. Attach curtain hardware on the inside of the door (we used café-curtain brackets and rods), and hang the panel. Platters and large plates are often wider than your cabinet shelves are deep, so stand them up. Keep plates from sliding with a strip of narrow molding glued to the shelf with wood glue, below left; finishing nails secure it completely. A platter, below right, is stabilized by a dowel placed a few inches above the shelf, attached to the cabinet with brass barrel fittings normally used for shirred curtains.

ARTIFACT BOXES Protect seldom-used china with adequate padding. This box, inspired by museum-style artifact storage, is simply put together. Line the bottom of a small, rigid cardboard box with Bubble Wrap. (Avoid plastic boxes, since the material prevents airflow and can cause moisture to build up.) Cut cardboard dividers, or use the inserts from liquor boxes. Wrap items in Bubble Wrap or paper, and place one in each slot. Sturdier items, like brass candlesticks, may be set in their compartments without any padding. Put a photo or detailed description of the objects on the outside of the box.

CHINA CASES Padded, zippered pouches made for holding china can protect it in storage, but they don't make finding a particular piece easy. The more you handle your china, the higher are the chances you'll have an accident. Reduce handling by labeling the cases (use string to attach a tag to the zipper pulls, left) so you don't need to open every one of them to find an item. Then store your china in cases on a low shelf to ensure that they can't fall far.

FELT PADS To keep china lustrous, protect it even while it sits on the shelf. When dishes are stacked, the bottom of one can scratch the one beneath it; placing felt rounds between them eliminates abrasion. Buy separators at housewares stores or cut rounds just smaller than the plates from felt or acid-free paper.

ARMOIRE FOR DISHES   If you find your china collection growing faster than your storage space, an armoire in the kitchen or dining room can provide the extra shelving you need and add to the aesthetic charm of the room. This European painted pine armoire from the late nineteenth century makes an elegant display case for antique porcelain, china, and glass. The custom-built cubbies give order to the collection: The pieces are accessible and the overall look is clean and uncluttered.

FELT TRAY Flatware dividers make organizing your forks, spoons, and knives a simple task, but they are often made of hard metal that can scratch precious silverware. Make your own soft silver tray by sewing together strips of sturdy industrial felt to fit your silver and your drawer.

FLATWARE DRAWERS Whether it's stainless steel or sterling silver, the flatware you use every day should be kept in a spot where it's easy to reach and to put away. The silverware drawers at left, built into the big kitchen island at Turkey Hill, are lined with silvercloth (antitarnish fabric). Even the most organized cook may find herself hurrying when it's actually time to put the food on the table. Keep serving pieces together in their own drawers, below, and spread them out generously to ensure that you'll always find exactly what you need.

A knife block on the counter may seem less than practical if space is limited. But keeping knives in a drawer presents another problem: When you pull open the drawer, knives spin and crash into one another, dulling the blades and increasing the odds of your hurting yourself. Line your knife drawer with artists' drawing-board liner. Its slightly rubbery surface keeps knives stationary and wipes clean easily. Cut it to size with a utility knife, below, and anchor it to the drawer bottom with double-sided tape.

WASHABLE LINERS Lining drawers can be done simply with a soft fabric, such as the fleece shown here, which is held in place by self-stick Velcro dots. Cut a piece of fabric to fit the bottom of the drawer. Apply the soft dots of Velcro to the underside of the cloth, and the corresponding rough dots to the drawer. Position the fabric in the drawer, and press the dots together. When necessary, the liner removes for washing.

MAKING A RACK

For this rack, you will need a half-inch-diameter stainless-steel tube, six feet long; two threaded eyebolts with nuts; two rubber caps; four screw hooks with anchors; heavy-gauge beaded chain and four brass couplings; and metal S hooks. Drill holes through the tube, one at each end, three inches from edge; insert an eyebolt in each hole and screw on the nuts. Slip rubber caps over ends of rod. To hang the rack so it won't swing, drill two holes in the ceiling for each end of the rod, placing each pair three feet apart; insert screw hooks, using the correct anchoring method for your ceiling. Attach brass couplings to each end of two lengths of heavy-gauge beaded chain, and slide the chains through the rod's eyebolts; hang each end on the ceiling hooks. Adjust the height of the rod by shortening the chain with wire cutters. Pans should hang low enough for you to lift them off their hooks without standing on tiptoes but high enough so you won't bang into them. Slide pot lids over handles and hang pans and utensils from S hooks, below.

HANGING POTS

When Martha redesigned her kitchen at Turkey Hill, some features were fine-tuned and others were changed altogether; one thing that remained the same, however, was the generous overhead hanging rack for her extensive collection of copper pots and pans. Besides keeping pots in view and easy to reach, hanging them overhead frees up cupboard space.

WALL RACK A short rail and several S hooks make a handy small rack for kitchenware if your space is limited or your ceiling is too high for suspending a rack. Handrails are better than towel bars for this job because they support more weight. Look for them, in sizes from twelve to thirty-two inches long, at surgical-supply stores. Metal S hooks are available at most hardware stores.

SUPERSHELF Look at how much this wall unit holds. For a unit this size, you will need two 10-by-12-inch brackets with cleat notches (see templates on page 137), a 32-by-12 inch top shelf, a 28½-by-4-inch bottom shelf, and a 30-by-3-inch cleat (a board that acts as a horizontal brace attached to the wall), all cut from ¾-inch-thick lumber; a ½-inch-diameter chrome bar, 27¾ inches long; and metal S hooks. Sand front edges of shelves and ends of top shelf to round them. Mark positions for bar and bottom shelf on inside of brackets. To hold bar in place, drill half-inch-diameter holes halfway through brackets. Place cleat in notch of one bracket, outer sides flush; drill screw holes with a countersink combination bit and screw in place from the back. To attach lower shelf, drill screw holes as before and screw bracket to shelf from outside. Attach other bracket in the same way, first placing bar in holes, then screwing cleat and shelf in place. Center top shelf on brackets, back edges flush and ends overhanging about one inch; drill screw holes and screw in place. Fill all screw holes with wood filler; sand smooth. Paint. To attach shelf to wall, drill three holes in cleat using countersink combination bit, centering one hole and drilling others close to a bracket. Making sure unit is level, attach it to wall with the appropriate anchors. Fill holes in cleat, and sand. Touch up paint.

STACKING SKILLETS   Nesting pots and pans saves space in a cupboard—but you should take measures to prevent them from damaging each other. Protect stainless-steel interiors by inserting circles of felt between pans. Nonstick surfaces are protected just as well by soft paper towels. For seasoned cast-iron skillets, use coated paper plates, which won't soak up oil.

POTS WITH LIDS   Eliminate the time-wasting search for the lid that goes with the pot. Here are two ways to keep them close together: Insert a wooden peg rack into a cupboard, and line up the lids vertically; or attach a graduated rack to the door, and stow lids as shown, the largest at the bottom, the smallest at the top. Enamelware is easily scratched, so insert felt circles, cut to size, between nesting casseroles. Use coffee filters of various sizes to protect smaller containers. A wooden tray holding pots slides out for easy access.

BAKEWARE ORGANIZER   A small cabinet seems spacious when neatly arranged. Stack cookie sheets on a shelf to create a handy sliding "drawer." Underneath, upend baking pans, trays, muffin tins, and other relatively flat objects between metal dividers. These dividers can be purchased at hardware and housewares stores. Also try organizing by type—deep trays in one slot, shallow trays in another, flat metal baking sheets in the next, and molded metal sheets, like muffin tins, fitted together, in the last.

Appliances used daily, such as your coffeemaker and toaster, probably never leave the counter, so dedicate the space around them to activities related to their use. Before breakfast, group jam and butter on a small tray to be whisked to the table in one trip. If space is tight, keep the counter clear for whatever appliance you need. In the evening, the coffeemaker and toaster can make way for the food processor. The key is that everything on the countertop can be stowed at a moment's notice. The only permanent resident is the outlet, ideally a grounded (three-pronged) one with ground-fault interrupt (GFI) to prevent shocks.

TOWEL HOOKS Dish towels may reside in the kitchen, but when in use, they are usually bunched up—still damp from wiping the counter—and looped through the handles of refrigerator and oven doors, where they never dry thoroughly. Sew a loop of twill tape on the end of a towel, and you'll always have a way to hang it when it is wet. A few hooks mounted on the wall or the side of a cabinet will give towels room to dry.

PREPARATION AREA Countertops should be as clutter-free as possible, since cooking takes up a lot of room. Preparation almost always has several stages, so devote space to each task along the way. Here, a wire sink colander holds just-washed produce, reducing crowding on the countertop. Keep a big area clear for chopping; Martha likes to use a large cutting board that is nearly as deep as the countertop itself and stow it when it's not in use. Note the ingenious under-shelf storage of the rolling pin, a kitchen implement that is usually a challenge to keep handy but out of the way.

WALL STORAGE Never forget your walls when organizing your kitchen—a small blank spot may be just the space needed to mount your favorite tools. A row of hooks or pegboard mounted on the wall to the side of the stovetop offers easy access to items that would otherwise be lost in a jumbled drawer, such as cheese and ginger graters. The hooks can also support a wire basket where fresh ingredients such as ginger and garlic can be stored.

SPICE STAND Assembling in advance all the spices you'll need not only saves time but also keeps you from getting halfway through a recipe before you notice you're out of oregano. A cake stand provides the stage for spices in a particular dish or for seasonings you use all the time.

BY THE STOVE When cooking, you want what you need nearby and what you don't need out of the way. Keep commonly used tools in a crock or masonry jar.

Here, wooden and plastic implements are in one crock, metal in another. Group basic ingredients such as olive oil, vinegar, salt, and pepper on a small tray, to catch errant drips. Salt and pepper for cooking are best kept in small open cups, making it easy to season food as it cooks. To store olive oil for cooking, use a small bottle that you can refill as needed, and keep your main supply in a cool, dark cabinet or pantry.

To keep your kitchen sink uncluttered, shop flea markets or housewares stores for pretty little trays to hold sponges, brushes, and dish and hand soap; the trays will minimize spillover to the countertop, and when you need to clear the sink, you can remove multiple small items quickly. Find a glass bottle in which to decant your dishwashing liquid—the main supply can hide under the sink. A basic tenet of space saving: Let items serve double duty. When you have only a few things to wash, use a wire rack atop a sheet pan to drain dishes. They vanish into the cupboard after dishes dry, leaving valuable open work space near the sink.

PULL-OUT BOARD

When chopping, eliminating the space between the cutting board and the trash pail will also eliminate trips from counter to trash can and prevent food scraps from wandering where they don't belong. This cutting board rolls out from behind a false drawer front and is positioned above a pull-out garbage bin, so the cook can chop food, then palm-sweep the mess into the pail below.

KITCHEN IN AN ARMOIRE   In the time since most clothes moved out of armoires and into closets, armoires have been free to move into other rooms. Their generous size can accommodate a kitchen's worth of supplies. Although this charming Danish pine armoire, opposite, dates from the 1860s, it looks right at home in a modern kitchen. A steel closet pole replaces the original wooden one, and pots and pans are suspended from it by S hooks. On the shelf below, pot lids, a crock of wooden spoons, and other essentials share space. Every inch of this armoire was put to use, including the doors with their linen-covered panels: The bulletin board is made from Homasote; the other three boards are plywood. Linen was stretched over them and secured in back with a staple gun. The mini laundry bag, left, was made from two dish towels. Install two grommets at the top, and hang the bag from cup hooks.

SPICE DRAWERS   Every cook deserves a well-stocked collection of spices, but you may not have a wall big enough to accommodate a traditional spice rack. These simply constructed drawers prop spices slightly upright to make searching for the ginger a snap. Handles were attached to plain wooden boxes for drawer pulls. Each row of jars rests on two dowels (these are three-eighths inch in diameter)— one near the bottom, the other a little farther back and higher. To install, drill holes the diameter of the dowels in the sides of each drawer, and slide the dowels through, securing with wood glue.

For a kitchen that doesn't have a pantry, a flea-market find like this nineteenth-century wooden cupboard will do the job. Deep shelves hold staples and shield them from light, an important factor to consider for oils and other delicate ingredients such as nuts, baking extracts, and chocolate. Hooks are installed on the doors for various hanging items. The top makes a good shelf for pitchers and large canned items.

PANTRY IN A DRAWER On the shelves of a full pantry, boxes standing four or five deep will block access, and bags of grains or flour can topple over. Solve both problems by also using shallow drawers as your pantry. These are perfect features for a pantry because their proportions allow all of the contents to be arranged in a single layer and displayed at once. Bags of rice in the top drawer are carefully labeled according to the type and the date of purchase.

AIRTIGHT STORAGE Baking needs such as assorted sugars, chocolate squares, and decorating supplies should be stored in airtight glass jars; after the package is opened, marzipan should be placed in a well-sealed plastic bag. To keep track of a container's contents, enclose part of the package's paper label.

SHELF LIFE

· Hardy vegetables, such as sweet potatoes, pumpkins, and winter squash, can be stored in the pantry for up to a month. So can potatoes and onions—but not together, as they cause each other to spoil.

· Beets, carrots, and celery require temperatures between thirty-two and forty degrees and should be refrigerated, as should most fruits.

· Oils, with a few exceptions, keep well in the pantry even after they've been opened, as long as they're stored in closed, lightproof containers. Delicate nut oils should be refrigerated, as they can easily go rancid.

· Any vinegar stores well in an ordinary pantry cupboard.

· Sugar can get hard and lumpy in high humidity, so it's best to transfer it to an airtight glass jar. Flour, grains, and beans need similar handling. The best jars for dry ingredients are wide-mouthed—the openings let you dip in with a measuring spoon or cup.

· Dried pasta looks great in airtight glass jars but it will store equally well in its original packaging.

· Nuts and dried fruits can be placed in airtight containers or left in original wrappers. If you use nuts only rarely, freeze them; they will last up to a year.

· Baking staples such as extracts and leavenings can be kept in their original packaging and grouped together on shelves for easy access.

· Both canned and bottled goods can be stored as they come; unless they have an expiration date, they will keep for several years.

· Always keep dried herbs in airtight, lightproof containers. If your pantry is a separate room that is both cool and low in humidity, you can hang fresh herbs there to dry.

SPICE APOTHECARY   Stash your precious spices away in a trim little cabinet recycled from a vintage medicine chest. Start with an old wooden medicine cabinet from a tag sale or flea market. Remove the mirror, leaving the door frame intact. Refinish the cabinet and door, if desired. Cut a panel of one-eighth-inch-thick lauan plywood to match the dimensions of the mirror. Attach adhesive-backed cork to each side of the plywood. Paint the cork using a color that blends with the cabinet or wall. Glue or tack the corkboard to the door in place of the mirror. Mount the cabinet on the wall.

Let your kitchen windowsill be an indoor greenhouse. A large, inset window that gets lots of light works best. Measure depth and width of window frame, subtract a half inch from the width; have half-inch-thick glass cut to that size for each shelf (for maximum sunlight). Have the edges sanded. With a level and a pencil, mark where shelf supports should go, starting from top of frame. For supports, cut molding—plain, as shown, or a more ornate type— into lengths to fit the depth of the frame (two for each shelf); sand the ends smooth. Drill three holes (just bigger than the head of a wood screw) in each support. Hold a support against a mark, place a drill bit through one hole, and drill a starter spot into the frame. Repeat for the other holes, then countersink the screws. Repeat for the other supports. Fill holes with wood putty, sand, and paint the supports. Once they are dry, attach a felt dot or plastic glide to the top of each support at the ends, and rest the glass on top.

ENHANCING A CUPBOARD Mass-produced cabinets take on custom character with the addition of brackets and shelves. Here, four matching brackets—two right side up, two upside down—expand the usefulness of a stock double-door cupboard. A narrow shelf tucked underneath is the perfect spot for spices. Below it, a dowel between the brackets holds dish towels. At the top, a flat horizontal strip keeps platters in place. Covered in a few coats of paint, the multipart cupboard looks like a single piece of cabinetwork. Choose a bracket style from the templates on page 137.

Storing heirloom recipes in a book will keep them organized and protect them better than keeping them in a box. Use pH-neutral material and separate the acid-containing cards. If an ancient recipe is actually beginning to crumble, spray it with deacidifying spray and place it next to buffered paper (which offers physical support and absorbs acids). To create the slots, below left, mark lines for the pocket openings, centering and spacing them so the top of one card won't overlap the one above. Make the bottom slot at least as far from the bottom of the page as the height of the card. With a utility knife and metal straightedge, cut slots; use a self-sealing mat (at art-supply stores) to protect the pages underneath. To attach envelopes, below right, cut each envelope so the back is the same height as the card and the front is one inch shorter. Starting with lowest slot on page, line up top edge of envelope's front with slot; glue in place below slot. Tape the back above the slot. Proceed with next envelope. Once envelopes are in place, use archival-quality adhesive to affix them to one another. To install a photo, place it on the page, and mark each corner lightly with a pencil. Cut diagonal quarter-inch-long slits about one-quarter inch from each corner; insert corners of photos into slits.

COMPUTERIZED RECIPES

Recipes don't have to reside in boxes or notebooks. Store your old and new recipes on your computer, and in seconds you can find what you're looking for, whether specific ingredients or entire recipes. Print a recipe, and you have a kitchen copy that may be freely spattered with oil. Make easy adjustments to a recipe: Tinker with the cooking time or temperature, correct the seasoning, or adjust the ingredients. Best of all, you can add new recipes without the chaos of scattered pages and mismatched cards.

A word-processing program is the simplest way to access and print your recipes. By creating electronic folders, you can customize the setup to your needs. For instance, you can place all the recipes into one folder labeled "recipes"; the computer can even alphabetize them by name. Or you might categorize them by food type ("chicken recipes"), by country of origin ("French recipes"), or by course ("dessert recipes"), making a separate folder for each. If you want to take your filing system to the next level, there are computer programs that will organize your recipes for you, give you a recipe-search option, and generate recipe-specific shopping lists and nutritional analyses. Some will even convert a recipe for the number of people you're serving or from metric to U.S. units. Once organized in your computer, recipes share a uniform style. And passing them on through generations has never been easier; print your family favorites, slide them into binder sheets, and make a cookbook—or simply e-mail them to the lucky recipient.

RECIPE HOLDER

If you cook, it has happened to you: You're up to your elbows in cookie batter and you try to refer to the recipe card—only to find that it has slid off the counter and under the fridge. Instead of repeating that performance, keep your recipe cards off the countertop and in clear sight with a makeshift card holder: Place a fork in a glass or jelly jar, then slide the card between its tines.

LAMINATING CARDS

Handle favorite recipes without worry of spills or splatters: Laminate them, and you can just wipe them off. Print recipes two to a page on colored paper, below, one on top, one on the bottom. We color-coded our recipes, using orange for side dishes, yellow for appetizers. Cut each sheet in half; laminate the cards. Punch holes in the upper-left corners; string onto a loose-leaf ring.

chapter two

MAY 1996

JUNE 1996

SEPTEMBER 1996

OCTOBER 1996

NOVEMBER 1996

DECEMBER 1995/JANUARY 1996

FEBRUARY 1996

MARCH 1996

APRIL 1996

JUNE 1996

JULY AND AUGUST 1996

SEPTEMBER 1996

OCTOBER 1996

NOVEMBER 1996

LA BOHÈME

PARKE-BERNET GALLERIES

FRIBOURG

FURNITURE

APRIL 15 · 1950

LIVING ROOMS

EVERY HOUSE HAS MORE THAN ONE LIVING ROOM. THE AREAS WHERE FRIENDS and family naturally gather or relax aren't always dictated by where the sofa and coffee table are placed. But as people come together, things accumulate too. The coziness of living rooms can be their undoing: Their very comfort encourages us to fill them, sometimes to overflowing, with all the things we love to have around us—books, art, photographs, music. Adequate shelving is a necessary start, and once the bulk of your treasured possessions is filed away, boxes, baskets, and even footstools can pick up what's left over. For any lingering trouble spots, unexpected solutions can create a lasting peace.

BOOKS

SHELVES

ART & PHOTOS

MUSIC

TELEVISIONS

BOOKS

SHELF UNIT No matter the size or shape of a living room, unless you have the rare spartan aesthetic, a case can be made for filling an entire wall with shelves. Shelves don't take up space so much as create it. A generous shelf unit doesn't need to be deeper than fifteen inches to accommodate years' worth of accumulated books and possessions, and it gives the room a welcoming, studious quality at the same time. When you frame a wall of windows with shelves, as in this sunny living room, they can be connected by window seats for reading and star gazing. For details on how this shelf unit was constructed, see page 136. When you hang shelves, determine the composition of the wall by drilling a small test hole. Use mounting hardware recommended for the type of wall. Place shelves carefully—as you would hang a picture—in relation to the size and shape of the wall. When designing a framed unit of shelves, measure the objects that are going into it: books, vases, prints, or plates. Adjustable shelves are accommodating and versatile; if shelves are to be unmovable and fixed, build them at a variety of heights. And while you're taking the trouble, build more shelves than you think you will need; there is no such thing as an extra shelf.

LIBRARY TABLE Martha knew that an ordinary living room setup would be dwarfed by the Great Hall at Skylands; the room measures twenty-eight by forty-two feet. She planned the room around this nine-foot-diameter table, which serves as a casual horizontal library. Most of the books are about Maine and design.

FINIAL BOOKENDS Some bookends are no match for your volumes—they can hold books in place one moment and come crashing off the shelf the next. Architectural and drapery-rod finials affixed permanently to the shelves offer a polished solution. Finials are available in a range of shapes from housewares stores, restoration catalogs, and lumberyards. The drapery type comes with screws set inside; a plain wooden architectural finial will require that you drive a headless double-ended screw into center of base with pliers far enough so the other end won't go all the way through the shelf. Paint finial to match shelves. Before screwing in, drill a pilot hole.

BOOK STACKS Books are objects of beauty and deserve artful arranging. Alternate vertically shelved volumes with horizontal stacks; custom-built shelving, like the units here, can include a few narrow horizontal spaces just for holding extra-large books. When you run out of space (which is inevitable in an active reader's library), books stacked neatly in the vicinity of the shelves will look right at home.

SHELF CONSOLE   Even the tiniest front hall has room for a wall-hung, double-shelf console to keep ins and outs in order. The upper shelf extends beyond the brackets (see templates on page 137), and the lower one nests between them, providing a discreet space for mail. A small hook keeps often-used keys at hand.

GRADUATED SHELVES   Graduated shelves winningly make space for both large and small objects. They also fill a wall with storage without looming over the room. To unify shelves of different sizes, use appropriately scaled brackets with matching profiles. Here, the deepest shelves double as display and storage spaces. Narrower shelves hold small books and objects. All the brackets were notched at the back to accommodate the cleat, and the bottom ones were notched for the baseboard. See a selection of bracket templates on page 137.

To hold a collection of plants or to make an instant bar for drinks and hors d'oeuvres at a party, you can extend a windowsill by adding a hinged shelf above the apron, level with the sill. Select plywood the same thickness as your sill; cut it to the width of the sill and a depth of twelve inches. Paint the shelf before installing it. Attach the bottom of the shelf to the bottom of the sill with three hinges, one at the center, the others near the ends. For supporting brackets, below left, cut two right triangles from wood thin enough to lie flat beneath the folded shelf. Trim off the top outside corner of each bracket, for a shape as shown. The top of each triangle, once trimmed, should measure three-quarters of the depth of the shelf; the short side, three-quarters down the apron. Paint brackets before installing them. Hinge the short side of each bracket to the apron. When it's not in use, below right, the shelf lies flat below the window.

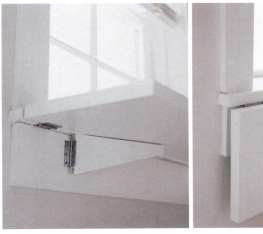

PLANNING A WALL Here's a foolproof way to plan a display of framed pictures without leaving a wall full of misplaced nail holes: Use low-tack drafting tape to hang templates, which can then be moved around until you find a pleasing arrangement. First, trace the picture frames onto kraft paper, and cut out the templates. Pull the hanging wire on the back of each frame taut, and measure from the top of the wire's arc to the top of the frame, below. On the matching template, measure in from the top edge this same distance to mark where the picture hook should meet the wire. Lay the picture hook on the template so that the bottom of the hook is on the mark; make another mark where the nail hole will go. Be sure to label all of the templates with a description of the pictures they represent. Use drafting tape to hang the templates on the wall. When you're satisfied with the placement of each template, hammer the nails through the picture hooks into the wall, right through the marks in the paper. Rip the kraft paper off, leaving the nails and hooks in place, and hang your perfectly arranged pictures.

SHELF LIFE   A narrow picture shelf made from decorative molding is a clean way to display a lot of art without making your wall look like a scrapbook. Once the shelf is in place, you can move framed pictures around without worrying about nail holes. These shelves were built into the wall, but you can achieve the same effect with narrow shelves trimmed in molding and screwed into the tops of cleats.

What do you do with family photos? The arrangement above a sofa, opposite, is composed of inexpensive eight-by-ten-inch frames in natural, pickled, and white-painted wood. The frames give consistency to pictures that differ in size and style; some are horizontal, others vertical. Begin a grouping like this with one row or a mini grid of four frames. A more uniform display, above, is achieved when all the pictures are taken with the same camera—here, a square-format one—or are printed at the same size and all the frames are identical and oriented the same. Either color or black-and-white film can be used.

STORAGE STOOL Any simple wooden box can be renovated as a footstool and used for storing photos, videotapes, or CDs, top right. For ball feet, saw unfinished drapery-rod finials off at the neck. Paint both the box and feet. Attach the feet, driving screws from inside the box. Attach a metal handle on each end. For the upholstered top, cut fabric just bigger than you want the finished panel to be, and cut batting just smaller than the fabric. Fold the fabric edges under; press. Center the batting on the box; place the fabric over it. Staple all layers at the corners and once or twice along each side. Cover the edges with grosgrain ribbon held in place with upholstery tacks; tap them in with a tack hammer, bottom right. A brushing with steel wool gave these shiny tacks a matte finish.

PHOTO STORAGE

Taking good care of your photos ensures that you'll be able to enjoy them for years to come. Clockwise from top left: One way to protect valuable prints from damaging exposure to light and dust is by storing them in a clamshell box, one with a lid that fits snugly into the base. Images are easily organized and protected in a photo-archive box. Storing slides in a file box will help you keep them organized and protected; here, they are grouped by theme in small boxes that fit in a larger one. Mismatched negatives and contact sheets become a thing of the past with this binder; since negatives are environmentally sensitive, be sure to use archival-quality plastic pages.

GRAY FLANNEL BOXES

Shoe boxes are perfect for stashing CDs, receipts, and photos, but their different sizes and colors make them look mismatched unless you suit them up for the job. You will need shoe boxes, men's suiting fabric, and polyvinyl acetate (PVA) adhesive. 1. Measure the perimeter and height of each shoe box. Cut fabric two inches longer than the perimeter and six inches wider than the height to wrap around the box. Coat one short side of the box with a light layer of adhesive. Press fabric in place, leaving a half-inch allowance for a sideways overlap at the start, and allowances of two inches along top and four inches along bottom. Wrap fabric around the box, applying glue to each side as you go. On the last side, fold under the last section of fabric and glue for a neat edge. Press extra fabric at the top into box on all sides and secure with glue. 2. Fold the remaining four inches of fabric under the box to cover the bottom; cut diagonal slits to each corner and trim away excess fabric. Glue fabric in place, folding last edge under. 3. Lay the lid on fabric, and cut a rectangle two inches larger on all sides (make sure the pinstripes run in the same direction as they do on the end of the box bottom). Apply glue to the top of the box, and reposition the top on the fabric. Fold excess fabric in, making hospital corners and applying glue to all surfaces to be covered. For a box-top tab, cut a four-inch-long piece of grosgrain ribbon, fold it in half, and glue the ends together. Glue tab to the inside of the lid at the center of one short side.

MUSIC STORAGE

The long-term durability of compact discs has yet to be proven, but they, along with vinyl records and cassette tapes, may last longer and sound better with proper care.

· If a CD plays smoothly, leave it alone. If the music skips or sounds distorted, your player's laser is probably having trouble reading the data on the disc. To clean discs, submerge in warm water, then clean with a soft cloth dabbed in a mild soap such as Ivory Liquid (wipe from the center out, not in circles). Rinse off soap and wipe discs dry with another soft cloth.

· Store records vertically—never flat.

· Make sure stored LPs don't lean to one side (add a book or two to keep them upright). Don't squeeze records together too tightly.

· Replace your paper sleeves with the acid-free or polyethylene variety.

· Clean vinyl with a record brush. Apply a record-cleaning solution in concentric circles so the fluid does not stick in the grooves.

· For especially filthy records, wash in distilled water and a mild dishwashing detergent, using a soft brush to get into the grooves; rinse with clear water. (Washing can damage some early laminated recordings.) Before washing, check to see if the label is colorfast.

· The ideal environment for CDs and records is an air-conditioned or centrally heated room with 40 to 60 percent humidity.

· Tapes are magnetic, so never store them on top of a speaker or in a cabinet with magnetic closures, which may cause the tape's particles to realign.

· Clean a tape player's heads with a cotton swab and pure (not rubbing) alcohol. Demagnetize them periodically using a store-bought demagnetizer.

STEREO STORAGE Stereos were meant to be heard, not seen. Here, a Guatemalan wooden cabinet, which is a more attractive storage center than many of the cabinets that are made especially for the purpose, camouflages a small sound system as well as several containers of compact discs and cassettes.

MUSIC STORAGE   Store-bought CD, tape, and record containers offer plenty of pleasing storage options. Customize music storage for your own needs. Clockwise from top left: CDs in wooden boxes are organized by genre; the label is a rubber stamp. Mend worn LP covers with archival tape before storing. Miniature file boxes can be tucked anywhere. Chicken-wire baskets offer see-through storage; boxes, whether of woven straw or black-and-white pasteboard, are stackable and discreet.

ALTERED CABINET If you want the TV to disappear entirely when you're not watching it, you need a television cabinet. The furniture designed for this purpose is often constructed on a mammoth scale, made unusually deep to accommodate the bulk of a large television. Happily, a trimmer piece, such as the vintage cabinet opposite, can be modified to fit a big TV. First, the back panel of the cabinet was removed. Then a low shelf was added to provide a space for the VCR and was finished to match the design of the cabinet. Once the shelf was completed and installed, the television was placed inside the cabinet and positioned far enough back for the doors to close normally. To make space for the back of the TV, which protruded from the rear of the cabinet, a hole was cut in the back panel before it was reattached, left. The back of the television now overhangs the dead space above the baseboard.

CONVERTED CABINET Almost any cabinet can be adapted to hold a television. Find one with a drawer large enough to hold the VCR, and add a swivel top and hinge the drawer front. For the swivel top, below left, you'll need a swivel mechanism and a piece of wood finished to match the cabinet. For the hinged drawer front, which drops down to reveal the VCR, below right, remove the drawer and disassemble. Return the drawer bottom to the cabinet and fix it in place. Refinish the inside of the drawer front, and reattach it with two small piano hinges. Cut a hole in the back of the cabinet for cables.

BEDROOM

THERE IS NO MORE PERSONAL PLACE IN YOUR HOUSE THAN YOUR BEDROOM.

Spend one night away from it, and you appreciate its familiarity. Ideally, the room itself is as soothing as a full night's sleep. But even a bit of clutter can feel distressingly like unfinished business when you turn out the light. Reevaluate your current setup: A nightstand that teeters with books, a laptop, and a knitting project calls for something roomier. An overstuffed closet begs for added shelves. Rethink the space to include underutilized spots, such as under the bed and below your hanging clothes, and you'll find room you never knew you had. And with all your possessions neatly tucked away, there's nothing left for you to do but count sheep.

NIGHTSTANDS

CLOSETS

DRAWERS

HIDDEN BOOKCASES Some bedrooms don't allow space even for a tiny nightstand on either side of a double bed. Pulling the bed away from the wall to accommodate a deeper headboard, opposite and left, creates discreet storage space and eliminates the need for separate bedside tables. This headboard is made up of two sideways-facing bookcases united by a continuous top and a smooth front. The narrow bookcases offer ample room for reading materials and alarm clocks, thus freeing the top of the headboard for reading lamps, flowers, and keepsakes.

WALL STAND In spite of its name, a nightstand needn't have feet on the floor. A wall-hung cupboard such as this one, found at a flea market, can hold all your bedside needs and economize on space. A medicine cabinet or shallow kitchen cupboard would serve equally well. The glass-paned door affords a view of the books in your bedside library while keeping them dust free, and the drawer holds small items such as change and medications secure and out of sight.

SKIRTED TRAY TABLE A skirt softens a night-stand—and conceals an extra space to stow books. Instead of the familiar fabric-draped drum table topped by a glass disk, we used a rectangular table with a tailored skirt and placed a metal tray (fresh-ened with paint) on top. The tray keeps the fabric clean, and its raised sides prevent small objects from slipping off. If the table beneath the skirt doesn't have shelves or cubbies, consider adding one or two.

BEDSIDE SHELF In a small room, a bedside shelf has no legs to bump into in the middle of the night. Here, tabletop and brackets were cut from one-inch-thick plywood. Make a pattern for the double, rear bracket by placing two copies of a template from page 137 back-to-back with a one-inch-wide strip of paper in the center. Cut the rear bracket from this pattern, and a single bracket for the center. Screw center bracket and then tabletop to rear bracket. Screw rear bracket to wall.

NESTING TABLES Commonly found be-side sofas, nesting tables make a flexible nightstand, especially in a tight bedroom. During the day, after you move paper-work and other items to your briefcase or desk, the two smaller tables can be tucked away, leaving more floor space open. Come bedtime, they can be pulled out to segregate drinks and snacks from audio and TV controls and to sort reading materials.

LIBRARY TABLE For nocturnal and early-morning strategists, like Martha, a tiny nightstand just won't do. To accommodate a laptop, a phone, a tray of refreshments, a reading light, and books, you need a generous surface. A library table or a harvest table with a drawer or two is well suited to carry the load. At Turkey Hill, Martha uses this drop-leaf table: By lowering a leaf and shifting the chair, she can transform the look from home office to bedroom sanctuary.

PLANNING CLOSETS Organize your clothes well, and you'll find you wear more of them more often. Here, three short rods have a bigger capacity than a single long one. Dresses, evening clothes, robes, and coats hang from the high rod at left; the low rod, thirty-four inches above the shelf, accommodates skirts and folded slacks; another rod thirty-seven inches higher holds blouses and short items. All rods are twelve inches from the back of the closet to provide hangers with two inches of clearance. Stacked cubbies double the space for shoes, and belts and hats are given individual hooks on the inside of the door. A mirrored panel inside the other door turns an open closet into a dressing room. Shelves in the tower on the side are adjustable thanks to peg-in-hole supports, below left. And no snags here: Smooth vinyl matting, usually used to protect drafting tables or artists' drawing boards, is cut with a utility knife to fit each shelf and fastened in place with double-sided mounting tape, below right.

BABY ARMOIRE A small armoire makes an ideal closet for a baby's clothes and accessories, especially one that is given extra shelves and painted bins that slide out like drawers. On the insides of the doors, a pivoting pants rack sorts baby blankets, a clipboard keeps doctor's recommendations (and small works of art) close at hand, and a cotton piqué bag collects tiny laundry.

FITTED CLOSET

A single closet rod leaves the space under shirts and skirts unused. Rods that take both short and long items into account leave no space empty and render resulting sections roomy. Once installed, these stainless-steel shelves can easily be adjusted without tools. If the sweater collection grows, another shelf may be added. Archival and metal boxes store small things, like gloves and socks. The step stool folds for easy storage. A hanging shoe rack, below, organizes shoes in a minimum of space.

TRUNK SPACE

To make better use of a closet with a single rod, hang short items with short and long with long; grouping items this way will consolidate the space below as well. Off-season clothing may be kept in a trunk or in generous-size boxes that slide right into the space underneath skirts and blouses.

SWEATER Knits should be folded, but if drawer space is tight, use the dry-cleaner's method for hanging: Fold sweater in half lengthwise (shoulder to shoulder); drape it over the bar of a sturdy wooden hanger. To protect against creases, slip tissue paper between sweater and bar.

SHIRT A freshly ironed oxford shirt stays virtually wrinkle-free when hung on a shirt hanger and given some elbow-room in the closet. Buttoning all buttons and straightening the collar keeps the shirt crisp until you're ready to wear it.

SKIRT With a skirt made of a dressy fabric, hanging is the best way to prevent creases, but you risk dent marks where the hanger clamps on. For protection, fold two pieces of felt over the waist of the skirt under the clips.

CAMISOLE Anything fragile belongs on a padded hanger. But something filmy, like a silk or chiffon camisole with spaghetti straps, is likely to slip off. Sew two buttons onto the hanger and position the straps on the inside of the buttons.

PADDED HANGER
Designed for delicate items, the soft, rounded arms prevent dents in the fabric.

TIE HANGER
This design keeps ties separate and unwrinkled.

SHIRT HANGER
Usually smooth wood, it is slightly curved to follow the natural slope of the shoulders.

WOODEN HANGER
Fold pants or sweaters over the sturdy rod.

SKIRT HANGER
Its movable clips can accommodate various-size pieces.

SUIT HANGER
A bar holds the pants in place; curved arms keep the jacket's structure.

TROUSER HANGER
Clamp hangers are good for dress trousers with creases (hang them by the cuff).

HANGING VS. FOLDING

The following items should be hung:
· Linen, rayon, or all-cotton blouses; they're wrinkle-prone
· Slippery silks and satins, which slide around in drawers
· Delicate fabrics that crush easily—raw silk, chiffon, velvet, taffeta
· Anything featherweight, such as tiny tank tops and dressy camisoles
· Pressed shirts, to keep them free of fold marks
· Suit jackets and blazers—pieces with a definite shape to maintain
· Pants with creases
· Anything with pleats
· Most dresses, especially tailored styles
· Warm jackets and overcoats
· Bathrobes
· Ties, on a special rack—knitted ones should be rolled and stowed in a drawer

These items do better folded:
· Knitwear—tops, pants, skirts, and dresses
· Any sweater—cashmere to cotton, cardigan to pullover
· Bias-cut and A-line skirts and dresses (hanging them can distort their shapes)
· Long evening dresses, particularly if weighted by ornamentation
· Cotton T-shirts
· Jeans, corduroys, and khaki pants
· Scarves and shawls
· Lingerie and socks
· Sweats and sportswear
· Stretchy synthetics

HOW TO FOLD A SHIRT Oxford shirts will travel better and stay crisper if carefully folded rather than being zipped up in a garment bag. Here are three simple steps to expert folding: 1. Button the shirt (except for cuffs), and place it face down on a flat surface, arms out to the side. Take one arm and fold it over the back, bringing a bit of the body of the shirt over, too. Then fold the arm back on itself and down at an angle, so it lines up with the vertical edge of the body. Repeat on the other side. 2. Bring the shirttail halfway up the back, then fold the bottom half up once more to meet the shoulders. 3. Flip the shirt over, and smooth any creases.

CLOSET ON WHEELS The space under your bed—home to shoe boxes, dust bunnies, and the occasional monster left over from childhood—can be put to sensible use with bins made by attaching casters to wooden boxes or drawers, opposite. Have a carpenter or an unfinished-furniture store build boxes, or use orphaned drawers from a chest or even wine crates. To determine the height of the box, measure from bed frame to floor, and subtract one-and-a-half inches (for clearance) plus the height of the casters. For each, you will need one box (painted, if desired), four casters with mounting screws, a twelve-inch-long piece of one-inch-wide cotton-twill tape, and two upholstery tacks. If the bottom of the drawer or box you're using is thin, reinforce the corners with triangles of thin wood attached with wood glue, on which to mount casters. Drill holes for casters with a bit slightly smaller than the screws, and screw casters in place. To make the pull handle, left, fold the twill tape into a loop, cut ends together, then fold raw edges over twice by three-quarters of an inch. Place folded ends inside box at center front, one inch below top. Hammer tacks through folded tape.

TREASURE CHEST The only way to improve upon the classic chest of drawers, below, is to customize each drawer to its contents, right. In shallow top drawers, a velvet lining, attached to poster-board backing with archival glue, gives plush support to delicate items such as scarves and jewelry. Use a deep drawer for sweaters and line it with cedar blocks. Use boxes to create removable compartments that comfortably fit your clothes, and make the fewest folds possible in order to reduce creasing. Save a drawer for khaki pants and jeans. Acid-free paper will protect clothes from splinters and acids in the wood.

CHAPTER FOUR

BATHROOM

AT HOME, THE BATHROOM IS ALSO A BUFFER ZONE: IT'S WHERE WE GO UPON rising before facing the rest of the world, and it gives us a bit of quiet before bed at night. Bathroom routines—hair combing, tooth brushing, face washing— let the mind wander and help to refresh us. The meditative mood is easily ruined by a mess. You can maintain the sanctity of the bathroom by reserving your medicine cabinet for only those things you use every day; banish all the other jars and bottles to nearby storage. Keep handy more towels than you think you will need, and you won't have to endure a shivering, wet walk across cold tile. Rude awakenings should be kept out of the perfect daydream.

CABINETS

TOILETRIES

TOWELS

DOWNSIZING Astringent, rose water, and hair spray often come in bottles that take up too much room in the medicine cabinet. These smaller ones hold a good supply and are easy to refill. Since they're all the same design, they reduce visual clutter as well. For safety and quick access, always label the bottles.

MEDICINE CHEST If opening your bathroom cabinet invites an avalanche of cotton balls, refit your medicine chest with flea-market bargains. Here, bobby pins stand in an eggcup, talcum powder is stored in a tin sugar shaker, and mouthwash is ready to be swigged from an old flask. Clean used containers thoroughly, and label any items not instantly recognizable.

DOOR STORAGE Combs, brushes, and toothpaste take up considerable space when laid horizontally on a shelf. Flat-backed self-adhesive cups on the inside of the door hold them more efficiently. Before pressing the cups in place, line them up between the shelves. To ensure the door closes, put thin items on the shelves in the spots where the cups will take some space.

SIDE TABLE A side table with drawer and shelf is an ideal repository for infrequently used products; both the drawer and the basket set below it keep the usual jumble of bathroom needs neat. Above the sink you can store everyday items you don't want behind closed doors.

OPEN BOXES Cubbyholes supplement the medicine chest. Hanging them with spaces between them gives you plenty of room to store soap, shampoo, extra face towels, and clean cotton balls and swabs both in and on top of the boxes. Each one is made from five pieces of three-quarter-inch-thick plywood. Each side is twelve inches long by nine inches wide; the back is a twelve-inch square. The four corners are mitered, and the pieces are glued with wood glue and secured with one-inch finishing nails. If carpentry isn't your cup of tea, you may want to avoid mitering. Instead, have the lumberyard cut the top and bottom boards ten and a half inches long and the sides twelve inches long. Glue the top and bottom boards to the inside edges of the side boards and secure with finishing nails. Glue on the back and secure with more finishing nails. Sand, prime, and paint the wood. The finished shelves can be screwed right into the wall through the back (center them on a stud or use a wall anchor) and the screw heads hidden with paint.

MEDICAL JARS Keep beauty supplies on view and at their most pristine in glass surgical jars. The jars have stainless-steel lids with easy-to-grab knobs and are available at medical-supply stores. Here, a tall, narrow jar holds a hair-trimming kit, and shorter ones keep cotton swabs, cotton balls, sponges, and soaps at the ready.

FIRST-AID KITS When you need first-aid supplies the most, you're usually not in the best frame of mind to search for them. A well-stocked first-aid kit, top right, keeps the items you need handy. Bandages, adhesive tape, gauze, and scissors to cut them with are always useful. To clean wounds, keep hydrogen peroxide or isopropyl alcohol (and cotton balls or swabs to apply it) on hand; antibiotic ointment will promote healing. A first-aid kit is also a good place to store pain relievers such as aspirin, ibuprofen, and acetaminophen. Color-code pill bottles with stickers, lower right, so family members can spot theirs instantly, reducing the chance of ingesting the wrong one.

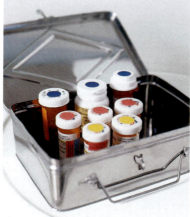

MEDICINE & COSMETICS

Although it seems counterintuitive, usually the worst place to store medicine is in the medicine chest. The buildup of heat and humidity in most bathrooms can cause medicines to lose their potency and expire before the expiration date on the label. Cosmetics can breed bacteria if they're not replaced every so often.

· Unless you're taking a prescription medication that will be running a short course, store all medicines in a cool, dry place.

· Most medicine-bottle caps are child-resistant, not childproof. Keep all medicines out of children's reach.

· Don't transfer pills and tablets from their original bottles into other containers; doing so increases the chance that you will take the wrong medicine or take your pills at the wrong time.

· The best way to dispose of medicines when they expire is to flush them down the toilet or grind them up in the garbage disposal.

· Any cosmetic product that changes color or develops an unfamiliar odor should be discarded.

· Clear out aging and underused products at least twice a year. Throw away eye makeup after three months of use. The eyes are more susceptible to infection than other parts of the body.

· Keep cosmetic containers tightly closed when they're not in use.

· Keep makeup out of sunlight.

MARTHA'S DRESSING TABLE Martha designed her East Hampton master bathroom in shades of white for a look both immaculate and full of light. The vanity is a zinc-topped 1930s farmhouse pastry table; set in front of a sunny window, it affords natural light for applying makeup. A freestanding mirror with a small base saves space. Toiletries, cotton balls and swabs, and soaps sit in individual trays that keep the tabletop from looking cluttered. Taller items are kept in the back.

TOWEL CABINETS Martha found the cupboard she now uses as a towel cabinet, opposite, in a bedroom of her East Hampton house when she moved in. The white wood and glass doors are right at home in the bathroom there. Towels kept on top can be grabbed as needed. A larger supply is enclosed in the cabinet for longer storage. Open shelves on the sides hold glass jars full of cotton and soap. The turn-of-the-century doctor's-office cabinet at left was bright pink when Martha spotted it in a junk shop. Repainted, it matches the plush white towels it contains. The glass panels keep towels in view so that guests don't have to hunt them down.

WINDOW SHELF As long as you install it thoughtfully, an extra shelf for bathroom needs can go almost anywhere. These two shelves use the same style of bracket in two sizes (see the bracket templates on page 137). The shelf above the window is a stash for towels and other supplies; a narrow, scalloped wooden apron nailed below the front edge makes a graceful valance. Between the window and the door, a bracketed shelf sits on a cleat with a row of pegs. A strip of wood extends above the front edge of the shelf, forming a low rim that prevents items from tumbling off.

GUEST TOWELS

It's customary to welcome each houseguest with his or her own set of towels. If you are expecting a full house, distinguish the sets with ribbon trim. For each set (bath towel, hand towel, washcloth), choose colorfast grosgrain ribbons wide enough to cover the dobbies (braided or flat borders) on each towel. Press ribbon, and pin to front of towel to cover dobby, tucking ends under. Thread sewing machine with top thread to match ribbon, and use bobbin thread the same color as towel. Topstitch the ribbon all around.

TOWEL LADDER

After a few trips to the beach or pool, do you find every free railing and rack in the house draped with damp towels? Keep things tidy by hanging towels from the rungs of an apple-picking ladder propped against a bathroom wall or set on a porch so sand isn't brought indoors. To keep the ladder from slipping, attach rubber tips made for chair legs to its feet. You can also secure the top of the ladder to the wall with hooks and eyes.

ROLLING TOWEL

The rolling hand-towel loop was an excellent invention that has a place in the home even today. Simply stitch two linen hand towels together at both ends to form the loop. To install it, take a half-inch-diameter wooden dowel (you'll probably want to paint it with enamel first to seal the wood), and screw porcelain drawer knobs, below, into each end. Slip the towel loop over the dowel, and hang the dowel from hooks mounted in the wall.

MAKEUP TOWEL Your houseguests have gone, but they've left traces behind—smears of lipstick and mascara on your otherwise pristine white towels. Try this simple solution, which Martha uses at Skylands: Have some dark towels embroidered with the word "makeup," and include one with each guest's set.

POCKET WELCOME A simple but ingenious way to make your guests feel welcome is to provide them with a hand towel folded to create a sturdy pocket for toothbrush, toothpaste, and washcloth. No sewing is necessary. 1. Lay a standard hand towel face down, and fold up the bottom about a quarter of the way. 2. Turn the towel over, and fold in the sides so they overlap completely. 3. Flip the folded towel over again, and hang it over a larger towel on the towel rack. Fill the pocket with the aforementioned necessities or bath salts and other luxuries.

PART TWO

WORKING

HOME OFFICE

WORKROOMS

UTILITY ROOMS

STORAGE ROOMS

CHAPTER FIVE

HOME OFFICE

FOR SOME, A SMALL TABLETOP FOR WRITING LETTERS IS ALL THEY NEED. FOR others, a scale replica of the desk at the office, complete with in and out boxes, is essential to getting anything accomplished. Whatever your style, you can find the space. Insufficient drawers can be supplemented with pretty filing boxes. A pantry cabinet can provide storage space when hung above a desk. A burdened desktop may be relieved by tacking invitations and doctor's appointments to an attractive handmade bulletin board. And you may finally part the sea of bills, receipts, and documents flooding your desk if you create—and stick to—a simple filing system. Don't forget, you want the boss to be proud.

DESKS

BOXES & BINDERS

BULLETIN BOARDS

CLOTHESPIN MEMO RACK The home office opposite has all the essentials without a trace of clutter in sight. A laptop closes and moves to a shelf to make room for writing letters; a printer sits on a side table, leaving the desk clear. Antique glass containers and galvanized boxes store paper clips, stamps, and other supplies. Clothespins on an unobtrusive strip at eye level hold correspondence, a calendar, and whatever is relevant at the moment. To make the message center, left, drill a mounting hole in each end of a twenty-four-inch length of two-inch-wide lattice. With wood glue, attach seven wooden spring clothespins in an up-and-down sequence, letting the springs overhang the board. Spray-paint the whole thing and attach to the wall using the appropriate anchors (use a washer between screw head and board).

HOMEMADE BLOTTER A blotter protects your desk from exploded pens and dropped staplers. Cover a sixteen-by-twenty-inch art panel with art paper that's cut an inch bigger on all sides. Center panel on wrong side of paper; cut out corners, below. With bone folder, score paper along sides of panel. Apply craft glue to panel edges; fold paper over. Turn panel over, slip on two taut loops of elastic. Slide in a sheet of art paper, a quarter inch narrower than the panel on all sides. Keep extra sheets handy.

STATIONERY FILE Take a hard look at those stacks of paper amassing beside your computer desk: torn-open packages of letterhead, printer paper, address labels, invitations, greeting cards, personal stationery, even a collection of scrap paper. Tidy up by filing a selection of each into a sturdy accordion-style folder. Label each slot clearly and refill as needed with a new supply.

TAMING WIRES Don't get your legs caught in a tangle of electrical cords under your desk; mount a power strip to the underside of the desktop so the only cord that has to travel to the outlet is the strip's. Then mount a coated wire basket, available in housewares stores, beside the strip. Bundle lengths of wire with twist ties and arrange neatly in the basket. Tags identify which machine each wire comes from, to avoid mass unpluggings when something goes wrong.

KITCHEN OFFICE In Martha's East Hampton house, a mudroom off the kitchen doubles as a home office. A farm table with a durable galvanized aluminum top makes a sturdy and attractive work surface. The overhead office storage system is a wall-hung antique pantry cabinet with Homasote panels fitted into the back to create a bulletin board and message center. Desk accessories include a collection of classic American ceramics, among them a green pottery lamp.

This office occupies unused space at the top of the house. Wooden shelving is tucked into the eaves, and the desk, a cut-to-measure stainless-steel restaurant-kitchen table, fits below a dormer. Extra storage is provided by a flea-market cabinet fitted with casters. Clips hung on cup hooks provide display space for correspondence, invitations, and doctor's appointment cards. Wooden CD cubes, below, also store floppy disks. Painting the floor and ceiling white prevents attic claustrophobia.

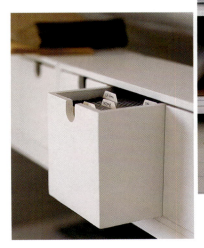

ARMOIRE OFFICE Every house can have an extra room if it's tucked into an armoire as this home office is, opposite. The original top shelf and pegs of this nineteenth-century Hungarian ash-wood piece, left, were kept in place; new shelves of one-and-a-quarter-inch-thick poplar were stained—and battered a bit—to match the old one. The desk insert, made of medium-density fiberboard (MDF), has a hinged front that serves as a desktop when open; the insert is screwed to the shelf it sits on, in the center. Wide cubbies were designed for letter paper; others are just right for envelopes or pencils. A bronze lamp illuminates the armoire; the cord runs out a gap between two boards, but you could drill a hole for it. Crisscrossing ribbon creates bulletin boards on the insides of the doors with a minimum of holes.

COVERING A DESK Cover the top of a desk with canvas, linen, or leather to protect it from wear and tear. Measure the tabletop, including its thickness; double the thickness and add this number to all sides. Cut fabric to this dimension. Fold a hem equal to the thickness of the table; press. Using a cloth-covered hammer, tack fabric to side of tabletop with upholstery tacks, below, at one-and-a-half-inch intervals. Begin at one corner and complete one side. Stretch the fabric and tack it at the remaining corners, folding under to make a vertical seam at each corner. Tack remaining sides.

LIBRARY DESK A wall-hung grid divides and conquers the monthly heap of paperwork and adds display space as well. The office-size desk is an old farm table fitted with a leather blotter. The office chair is dressed up with a fabric more suitable to a living room. When the laptop is shut and stowed in the space beneath the grid, the home office effectively closes shop for the day; the desk becomes a library table for reading or letter-writing. Beneath the desk, a regulation file cabinet stripped of its office-drab paint now gleams with a thick new top of green glass, and casters allow it to roll forward. Blond-wood cubbyhole boxes for organizing smaller supplies, right, are covered with felt on the bottom and sides to slide as easily as drawers. Dividers inside one keep small items from tangling with one another.

BEDROOM DESK A white enamel-top table with a blue enameled edge keeps the mood light, not officey. The chair, a flea-market find now painted grayish white, has a seat covered in Martha's favorite chintz. Mismatched china holds pencils, office supplies, and receipts; a rectangular metal pail holds correspondence. The shelf above the desk was made by attaching a readymade unit with slide-out box drawers to two pairs of metal brackets turned upside down to make bookends and dividers.

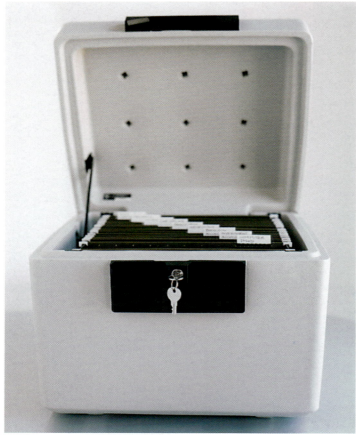

A HOME SAFE Keeping important documents in a fireproof safe is good protection against loss. These boxes have ratings based on the number of hours the interior will withstand the heat of a fire. A rating of one hour should be sufficient for the average homeowner. But even the most pickproof home safe can still be carried away—bolt it to the floor from inside the safe, left.

DOCUMENT STORAGE

· Use a safe-deposit box to store documents that are difficult to replace: birth certificates, wills, marriage and divorce papers, contracts, mortgage records, real-estate deeds, home-improvement receipts, paid bills for major purchases such as art or jewelry, stock or bond certificates, current home- and life-insurance policies, vehicle titles. Or ask your lawyer to keep them for you. Copies of them may be kept in a binder or accordion file in your house.

· For active records, such as unpaid bills, insurance claims, and anything related to your upcoming tax return, set up a two-drawer system in your filing cabinet. In the top drawer, set up files for all current financial paperwork related to bank accounts, credit cards, utilities, mortgages, insurance contracts, and so on. The bottom drawer should contain tax-related files. Reserve a nearby desk drawer, paper tray, box, or folder for your unpaid invoices.

· Once a bill is paid, the receipt should be filed in its proper place—a paid credit-card invoice, for instance, goes into a top-drawer file labeled with the name of that card. When canceled checks arrive, match them up with filed receipts, and staple the two together before refiling. Receipts and canceled checks with tax consequences, such as medical expenses or charitable contributions, should be filed in the bottom drawer with your current tax information.

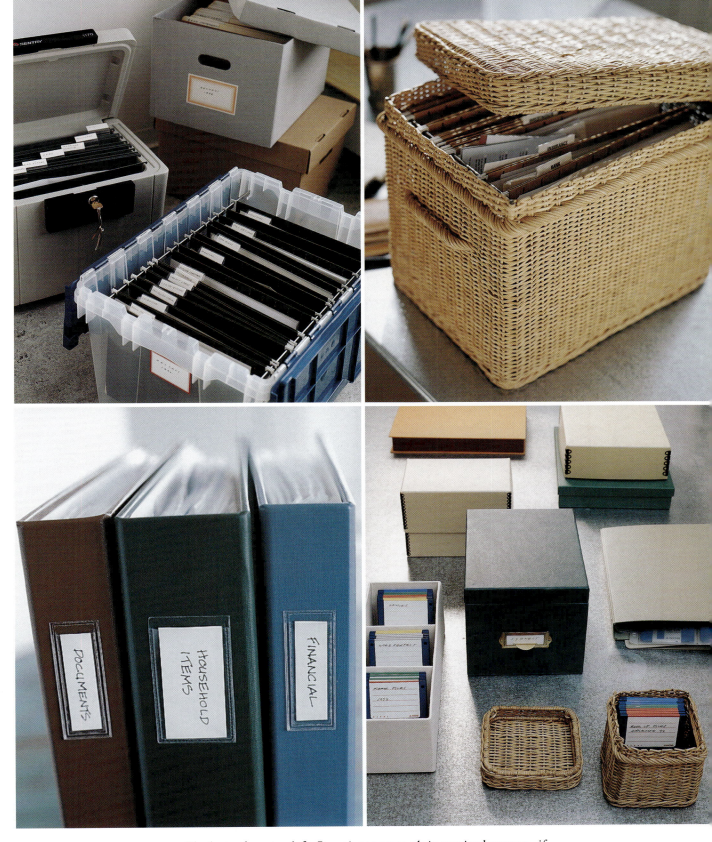

FOUR WAYS TO FILE Clockwise from top left: Organize tax records in moving boxes or—if your storage area is prone to dampness—plastic boxes. A straw basket is turned into a filing cabinet. Disks can be kept in small boxes or in plastic sleeves that fit three-ring binders. Keep copies of documents and a record of valuables and important possessions in loose-leaf binders.

Get organized—again and again—with these chalkboard drawers. The words can be erased as contents in each drawer change. Affix masking tape in square outlines to fronts of drawers or tins; cover each square with latex chalkboard paint, below. Let dry, and remove tape. To add a border, decide on its width, and place two strips of masking tape accordingly on opposite sides of the square; paint, let dry, and remove tape. Repeat with two other sides.

LETTER FILE Make a box for your correspondence with divisions: letters to answer, file, and save. This one was made from a pre-grommeted letter box with file folders and tabs. Leftover folders can serve for other office to-do's, such as invoices, bills, and lists of errands.

NO-DESK OFFICE

If you don't have a writing desk, use a wall near some shelves, and a section of the shelves, as your all-purpose organizers. At the far left of this bulletin board is a perpetual calendar filled in with birthdays and anniversaries. Pinned in place are photographs, postcards, letters to answer, and a roll of stamps hanging from a ribbon. The lower shelf of the bookcase is reserved for boxes holding writing materials, as well as desk accessories. The correspondence box, below, is large enough to hold letter-writing essentials—blank stationery, an address book, a pen, and stamps—but small enough to be easily transported from room to room or taken on the road.

FRAME BOARD A hard-working bulletin board is, quite literally, as pretty as a picture when covered with cheerful fabric, then placed in a frame and hung from a wide ribbon. The frame is painted to complement the fabric, which makes a perfect background for favorite photographs and letters, along with the more prosaic matters of life like the phone bill and the grocery list. You will need a large frame, new or from a tag sale, three-quarter-inch-thick Homasote cut to fit, fabric, a staple gun, and ribbon, below left. Cut a piece of fabric two inches larger than the Homasote on all sides; place face down on work surface. Center the Homasote over the fabric. Wrap one side of the fabric to the back and staple it to board, beginning with one staple in the middle of the side, one-and-a-half inches in from the edge. Wrap fabric over opposite side, and staple directly opposite the first. Repeat by stapling the fabric in the center of the other two sides. Continue stapling, working out toward the corners, always adding staples in pairs on opposite sides of the board, ensuring fabric stretches evenly. Place the covered board into the frame; secure with angle brackets at each corner, below right. Attach D rings to the back of the frame at the top corners. Loop ribbon through D rings, and hang.

RIBBON BOARD Stop taping that business card to the computer screen. Do not prop another party invitation, picture, or postcard against the desk lamp. Yes, one looks jaunty—but six? This project will provide the means to a cleaner, neater work space. The boards are Homasote covered in linen that was pulled taut around the board and stapled to the back. Let your creativity loose in weaving a pattern with ribbons, like the diamond pattern at top left, the tic-tac-toe pattern at center left, or the criss-crossed pattern at bottom left, inspired by the leaded windows of Victorian homes. The pattern above is modeled after a garden trellis. Use upholstery tacks (look for ones with intriguing designs) to secure ribbons. Tuck your cards behind the ribbons; you'll need few, if any, pushpins. Screw a picture hanger to the back, and hang the board on the wall.

chapter
six

ribbons

yarn

WORKROOMS

WHEN IT COMES TO TOOLS AND SUPPLIES, IF YOU DON'T GET ORGANIZED, YOU won't get your projects done. Ribbon ought to be arranged by color and easy to unspool; sewing supplies must be at the ready where you need them; potting soils need to be sorted and accessible. It doesn't take a lot of space to get organized, just a little creativity. An armoire given the right arrangement of shelves can make the perfect home for craft and art supplies; a shallow drawer can be outfitted with pretty dishware of different sizes and shapes to hold sewing notions; an under-trafficked corner in the garage can be converted into the ideal workbench for a gardener. With room to stretch out in, you just may find a new supply of inner creativity.

CRAFT
CLOSET

GARDEN

CRAFT ARMOIRE All it took to transform this blue-painted American Empire armoire into a crafts center, opposite, were a few extra shelves and dowels along the door. Metal standards, left, make new shelving simple; if you plan to hang things from the door, don't forget to cut the shelves a little shallower than the depth of the armoire so the door can close. A stepped shelf rests on the back of the highest shelf, making a deep space more useful and accessible; it was custom-made to hold jars of raw pigments in front and spools of ribbons behind. Tools—antique calipers, a printing brayer, a drafting triangle, scissors, a counter brush, and a funnel—hang from metal S hooks on the top dowel on the inside of the door. Other dowels have art paper draped over them (installing several dowels keeps papers from slithering away). Shelves in the middle hold rolls, sheets, and pads of paper, and bottom shelves hold wooden boxes.

PRETTY BOXES Boxes covered with beautiful paper make excellent containers for crafts supplies, and they will pleasantly remind you of the fruits of your labors. These boxes are covered with old documents found for a few dollars at a flea market; book pages or decorative papers would work just as well. Archival glue is the best adhesive for this project, but matte medium (a paint extender) can be used instead. Dilute the glue with a little water. Place a paper on the box, creasing it around corners. Remove the paper, brush a thin, even coating of glue on the back of the paper, and replace it on the box. Smooth it well with your hands or a bone folder. Keep adding papers, overlapping slightly, until the box is covered. Let dry completely, then brush another thin coating of glue over the whole box to seal.

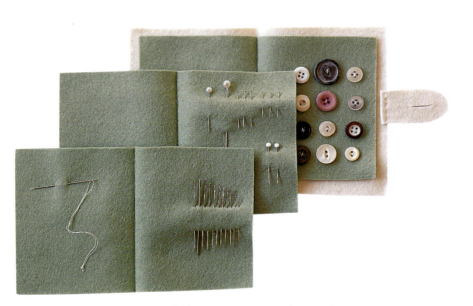

FELT SEWING BOOK

When you must mend something quickly, this little kit will help. Devote one page to extra buttons, one to pins, and another to needles threaded with your most-used colors. For the cover, cut heavy felt into two pieces, one five by seven and a half inches, the other two by one and a half inches. Sew a button on the center of one short end. Round one end of tab; sew straight end to the cover opposite the button. Cut a buttonhole slit in the tab. For the pages, cut lighter felt into rectangles four and three-quarter inches high and seven and a quarter inches wide. Fold pages in half; iron crease. Assemble book and close; bind it with embroidery floss in a blanket stitch, a half inch from folded edge.

BUTTON BOOK

Years may pass between the day you remove the extra buttons from a new jacket and the instant when you need to sew one of them on. To keep them from going astray, corral them into a convenient button book. Attach the button envelopes and thread cards to blank pages in a small ring binder. Use double-sided tape; it allows you to open the envelopes without removing them from the page. Write a little note alongside each button to remind you what clothing it belongs to.

SEWING DRAWER

A streamlined solution to a jam-packed sewing drawer: railway or airline dishware. These shallow ironstone or porcelain vessels come in a range of sizes that stylishly organize odds and ends. Sleek pieces can be found at yard sales and in thrift stores. Pull out the drawer and arrange in it as many dishes as you need. Use a pencil to trace their outlines on the bottom of the drawer, then affix each piece of china with double-stick mounting tape. Even when the drawer is in motion, the containers will stay in place.

If your thread is out of order, spread your colors out visibly, and you'll note the subtle differences between raw and burnt umber. 1. Cut quarter-inch-thick pine nine inches wide and seventeen inches tall. Drill half-inch-diameter hole in top center, two inches from edge; saw off top corners. Starting a quarter inch from bottom, mark seven lines, two and a quarter inches apart. 2. For shelves, cut seven nine-inch strips of skew-back molding. On widest side of each, starting three-quarter inch from the sides, mark six dots, one-and-a-quarter inches apart; score dots with a pushpin. To hold molding for drilling, place molding to be drilled in a ravine created by placing two other pieces side by side. Wrap tape around a three-sixteenths-inch drill bit a quarter inch from the tip. Drill holes at all dots; stop drilling when edge of tape reaches wood. Insert a three-sixteenths-inch dowel, two inches long, in each hole, securing with wood glue. 3. With wood glue, attach shelves, aligning bottoms with marks. Clamp in place and let stand until dry. 4. Apply primer and two coats of paint.

POTTING BENCH You may aspire to construct a true potting shed, but if you don't have the space, try this potting bench, opposite. Besides a sturdy, flat work surface, you'll need both natural and electric light; a nearby water source; good ventilation; warmth; and a roof of some kind to keep you dry and protect you from the sun. The bench should remain in place all year, so pick a spot that isn't needed for another purpose. Here, the bench was attached to the shelving unit at its right and given two legs in front for support. The backsplash, of burlap-covered plywood, also serves as a pinup board for garden designs, photo inspiration, and planting schedules. Potting soil, sand, gravel, peat moss, vermiculite, and perlite are stored in plastic bins of varying sizes, each with a metal scoop; a wheeled garbage can slides in and out as you need it. A plywood board with hooks stores trowels, dibbers, garden forks, claws, a ball-peen hammer to smash pottery into shards, and other tools. Old mason jars and pots, left, hold plant labels of metal and wood, plus chopsticks and pencils for making holes in soil for seeds and cuttings.

STORING POTS To ensure that your terra-cotta pots survive winter and emerge ready for spring planting, put them away properly. Thoroughly clean and dry them to prevent the growth of fungus and plant disease. Then lay them on their sides, one tucked inside another, in a shallow wooden crate, out of the freezing cold. Never stack pots; changes in temperature and humidity make them swell, causing them to stick together and guaranteeing breakage.

GARDENER'S APRON This linen apron keeps gardening tools at hand in specially sized pockets. You'll need raw linen and cotton-twill tape (preshrink both). Cut linen two feet long by eighteen inches wide—make the selvage edge one of the long sides. Lay it flat, selvage edge toward you. Fold selvage up six inches; iron crease. Fold hems in the two ends; topstitch in place. For pockets, stitch from selvage to fold; reinforce by backstitching at the selvage edge. This apron has five pockets: two are seven inches wide, three are three inches. For the sash, center apron on a three-foot-long piece of twill tape. Fold tape in half lengthwise to wrap over top of apron; iron. Topstitch tape to apron near bottom of tape.

TWINE DISPENSER Keep unruly balls of twine in line with big aluminum funnels, which serve as both organizers and dispensers. No need to drill; simply hammer a nail through each funnel near the top lip, attaching it to the wall of a shed or the back of a door. Place a ball of twine or string in each one; run the ends out the spouts.

HANGING STRING If you're the type to get tied up in knots when loose balls of string start to unravel, hang spools of twine and cord on knotted ribbons. Slide the ribbons so that the knots are hidden inside the spools. Then suspend them from ball-point hooks screwed into a wall in your work area.

POTTING CUPBOARD A vintage wooden cupboard provides handsome storage for gardening supplies. Perched on the back porch, it serves as a way station between house and garden. You can step out the door, slip into your gardening shoes, and head off with tools in hand. On your way back in, kick off your shoes and stash them and the tools without tracking dirt inside. Make room in the cupboard for houseplant and cut-flower supplies, too. Wooden boxes customize the space: One holds bags of fertilizer and potting soil, the other holds tools. Simply paint unfinished boxes with semigloss or high-gloss paint to withstand moisture.

GARAGE WALLS Take advantage of the unused space between exposed studs in your garage or shed to get your garden tools in order. Use bamboo rods and inexpensive brass barrel fittings, normally reserved for curtains. Cut the bamboo rods a quarter inch shorter than the space between the studs. For each rod, screw the threaded halves of two fittings to the inside of the studs, making sure they face each other exactly. Slide a barrel over each end of the rod, then screw the barrels onto the threaded ends on the studs. The rods can be easily removed so you can slip spools of string or wire onto them for easy dispensing. Common S hooks and spring clips from your local hardware store make the other rods ready for hanging tools and additional supplies.

GARDENER'S WALL A sheet of Peg-Board can convert a spare section of wall into a tidy gardener's catch-all. The mounted Peg-Board can be outfitted with wire brackets to hold shelves for pots, watering cans, vases, and larger supplies; wall hooks provide spaces for each and every kind of gardening tool. Keep miscellaneous boxes and baskets for future use visible but out of the way on the topmost shelf. The shelves and hooks can always be rearranged to suit your needs.

CHAPTER SEVEN

UTILITY ROOMS

EVERYBODY WHO APPRECIATES THE ART OF HOMEKEEPING UNDERSTANDS THAT a sparkling bathroom has the broom closet to thank. Utility rooms—those behind-the-scenes spaces that work to keep the rest of the house looking beautiful—can be anything from a full-fledged room to a designated corner of the house; all they're required to be is useful. A canvas curtain keeps air-drying delicates out of sight, even if your laundry area is in the kitchen; labeling shelves in a linen closet helps keep everything in its place. And a small mat and drying rack convert a hall into a wintertime mudroom. Don't use utility rooms as clutter depositories—keep them neat, and they will help you keep your home in order as well.

LAUNDRY ROOM

LINEN CLOSET

MUDROOM

BROOM CLOSET

A CLEAN LAYOUT   A laundry room should be clean and functional. This means water-resistant floors, a fresh paint job in white or a light color, and an adequate source of light. Martha's Maine laundry room, opposite, is bright and spacious and has two deep sinks. A washboard isn't necessary—or good—for delicates, but it's effective for sturdy items. Martha keeps several sorting baskets, one each for whites and pastel colors; dark colors; towels, robes, and other terry-cloth items that create a lot of lint; and heavily soiled clothes. A big, economical box of detergent was poured into a more accessible glass canister, left, along with the scoop that came in the box.

DELICATES   If you wash delicates in a machine, put them in a net bag to keep them from getting tangled with or snagged on other clothes. Instead of tumble-drying them, it's better to spread your delicates out on a clothesline or drying rack. Martha found this one, designed to be mounted on a wall, in her Maine laundry room. Because there is no wall convenient to the sink, the rack was screwed into a dowel and inserted into a pipe fastened to the lower wall. The rack can be folded and stored when not in use.

SORTING LABELS

With tags labeling each bin, there's no confusion when sorting laundry. If you only have room for two bins, start with the basic categories: lights and darks. Add bins as you need them: delicates, hand-washables, towels, sheets, bright colors, whites, heavily soiled items, and dry cleaning.

LAURY WALL

Adjustable wire shelving is convenient and waterproof; in this laundry area, one shelf is reserved solely for drying sweaters. Wooden boxes house supplies. Install a tension rod upon which to hang clothes as you take them out of the dryer; that way, they'll need only a light ironing or no ironing at all.

FOLDING SHELF

A shelf in the laundry room provides the perfect place to fold clothes fresh out of the dryer, but many small laundry rooms are already cramped with just the two machines. Making the shelf collapsible is the perfect solution; mount the shelf to the wall using collapsible metal brackets.

In Martha's East Hampton laundry room, she keeps her laundry supplies tidy and out of sight with built-in shelves and a curtain that can be pulled across them when the laundry is done. Mothballs and cedar chips are stored in canning jars, and little bars of soap are kept in airtight containers. Towels for drying hand-washables are stacked on one shelf. Special stain remedies are kept together in a galvanized metal box.

HIDDEN LAUNDRY ROOM

In this hallway laundry space, an unbleached-linen curtain moves on a hospital track so the washer and dryer can disappear. A space between the wall and cupboard leaves room for the track to continue to the back wall, so the curtain can be pushed entirely out of the way. Hospital tracking can be purchased from most hardware stores.

SHEETS AND TOWELS

In the ideal linen closet, opposite, everything is visible. Everyday items are easy to reach, and seasonal items, like baskets of beach towels and a quilt in a bedding bag, are on the top and bottom shelves. Drawers give delicate antique linens an extra level of protection from the outside world. Stacks of linens are spaced apart, allowing them to breathe and you to find what you need easily. Linens are grouped in categories: bedding for each bedroom; towels for each bathroom; sets of guest towels (bath towel, hand towel, and washcloth) bound together with ribbon, like gift packages. Label your shelves, left, to keep yourself honest when putting linens away: You'll be less likely to cram things where they don't belong.

PRESERVING FABRIC

Your antique linens deserve to be treated with care; line shelves or drawers with acid-free tissue paper to help keep the fabric from yellowing. Reserve shallow drawers for delicate linens. Stacked too high, they make a hospitable environment for bugs and mold. Use acid-free tissue paper to separate linens from the drawer and from one another.

NAPKIN SETS

You should never have to overturn the linen closet just to assemble enough matching napkins for a dinner party. Keep sets of napkins together by wrapping them in wide bands of cellophane. Secure with an adhesive label indicating the number of napkins.

FOLDING TOWELS   Keep sets of guest towels together, bound with twill tape or ribbon. When visitors arrive, transfer the bundle from the linen closet to the guest bedroom. Fold towels so edges are hidden and towels look fluffy and neat. 1. Fold the towel in thirds lengthwise. This is also the way to hang it over a towel rod; any monogram will be centered. 2. Fold it into a rectangle.

HANGING LINENS   Tablecloths hung on wooden hangers come out with fewer wrinkles. Place a sheet of acid-free tissue paper between the rod and the cloth to protect the cloth from the wood, and drape another sheet of tissue over the tablecloth. Attach handwritten tags to the hanger so that you can identify each tablecloth at a glance.

BLANKETS   Zippered cloth-and-plastic bedding bags protect blankets and quilts when not in use. Because the heaviest blankets spend so much time in the closet, the bags will keep them from getting dusty. The transparent plastic top makes it easy to identify the contents.

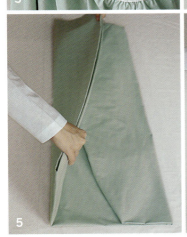

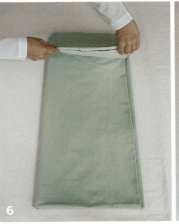

FOLDING FITTED SHEETS At last—a foolproof technique for folding a fitted sheet. These directions are for a right-handed person; if you're left-handed, use the hand opposite the one suggested. 1. With the sheet inside out, place one hand in each of two adjacent corners. 2. Bring your right hand to your left, and fold the corner in your right hand over the one in your left, so the corner on top is right side out. Next, reach down and pick up the corner that is adjacent to the one that was in your right hand (it will be hanging in front), and fold it over the other two; this third corner will be inside out. 3. Bring the last corner up, and fold it over the others so it is right side out. 4. Lay the sheet flat, and straighten it into the shape shown above. 5. Fold two edges in, folding the edge with elastic in first, so all elastic is hidden. 6. Fold the strip into a smaller rectangle. 7. Continue folding until rectangle is the size you want.

TASK CENTER Outfitted with pegs, benches, and cupboards, the mudroom opposite serves as a footlocker for the sports enthusiast, a potting shed for the gardener, a sort-and-fix center for the flea-marketer, and a bathing area for the family pet. A sink in a mudroom can handle jobs too messy or inconvenient for the kitchen: watering or spraying houseplants, or soaking linens. In keeping with the practical nature of the room, the sink and counter are seamless stainless steel. A high shelf sits on top of the peg rail and provides storage for seldom-used or seasonal objects. A ball of string for tying trash bags and newspapers and a chalkboard marked with frequently called numbers hang from multipurpose pegs. Simple triangular brackets and cleats, left, support shelves that organize a jumble of boxes, books, pots, and favorite postcards.

COOL PANTRY Kept at a cooler temperature than the rest of the house, the mudroom becomes a secondary pantry, ideal for storing cooking oils, wine, root vegetables, and flower bulbs waiting to be planted. Under the sink, a metal bin next to the one for recyclables holds vegetables that are best kept out of the light. Curtains of cotton shirting hide the bins and keep the area dark.

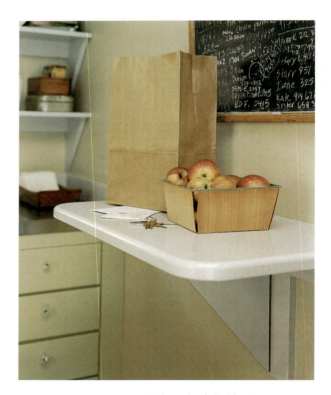

FOLDING SHELF A drop-leaf shelf is just the spot for unloading arms laden with groceries and mail. The top and brace are each mounted on the wall with a piano hinge that runs the length of the piece and provides stability.

MINI MUDROOM If you don't have an entire room to catch the dirt that everyone trails in, use a corner of a vestibule or hall, on a back porch, or on a landing at the top of the basement steps. Sealed natural-stone floors are slush-tolerant in winter, cool in summer, and low maintenance year-round. Keeping dirt at bay involves several mats: one outside the door and another inside. A chair rail and a high parallel upper rail hold pegs to accommodate family members of all sizes.

HALL BENCH This bench not only provides a place to sit while changing footwear, but also has handy cubbyholes—for towels to dry toes and mop up puddles, for socks and slippers to change into, for sports gear that needs to be gathered just before going outdoors. A thin lip of molding attached to the front of the bench at the bottom shelf keeps things from sliding out.

DRYING RACK   An accordion-style wine rack doubles as a compact dryer for wet woolens in wintertime, and can be collapsed and stored or used for swimsuits and towels during the summer. Around the holidays, it can return to its original purpose—storing extra bottles of wine.

L-SHAPED SHELVES   Even a small closet can pack a lot in: L-shaped shelves leave room at the front of the closet for standing or hanging long items like brooms and vacuum wands.

BOOT TRAYS   Sheet pans and cooling racks from a bakery-supply store make perfect portable drying racks for wet shoes and boots. (Boots can also be hung upside down to dry by slipping the heels between pairs of pegs installed close together.) Small pegs right next to the door can help you keep track of easily misplaced items like keys and a pet's leash, and they make a handy place to hang a flashlight.

To keep your old newspapers from slipping and sliding all over the floor between pick-up days, confine them to a recycling bin. Start out with a fourteen-by-twelve-inch wooden crate with slatted or solid sides. For mobility, attach four casters to the bottom of the crate. Paint the crate, and attach a two-inch metal cleat, centered, to the exterior of each side and a screw eye on the top rim. Before filling, run lengths of twine loosely across the box and through each pair of opposing screw eyes, then wrap it around the cleats to secure. Use the twine to tie the papers.

ALTERNATIVE BINS   Martha found these vintage American pickling crocks in various sizes at antiques stores and flea markets. A roofer made aluminum lids to fit and riveted on the handles. (To get the correct lid size, measure the crock's diameter and add about one inch.) Use the covered crocks to store garbage, recyclable bottles and cans, or even dry pet food.

SECURING TRASH BAGS Too often it happens that you deposit something heavy into the trash only to see the plastic liner collapse inward. Secure the bag to the can by folding it over the rim and clamping it in place with four metal binder clips evenly spaced around the circumference. The clip handles fold flat against the can and will be concealed by the lid.

KEY CORRAL Why not borrow this idea from innkeepers and hang everyone's keys in a box? That way, if someone needs to move a car or unlock a bike, there's no need to hunt for the key. This box of unfinished pine was painted white and given a porcelain knob. But an old medicine cabinet or cigar box can do the trick, too, with a few cup hooks screwed inside.

KEY BOARD Where are your keys? Here's where—on a linen-covered Homasote board. Wrap the linen around the board; with a staple gun, staple it to the back, securing it along one side first, then the opposite side, and lastly the remaining sides. To cover the staples, attach felt to the back with craft glue. Attach picture hangers to back. Mark spots for hooks with pins, and screw hooks into board. Nail the tags in place and insert labels. Hang the rack near your busiest door.

BROOM RACK

A neat broom closet, opposite, will certainly make you feel more optimistic about cleaning the house. Make sure it's stocked with only what you need and nothing more. Cleaning supplies are grouped by the room in which they're used. A towel bar mounted behind the vent on the door lets damp rags air out, and sturdy hooks on the back of the door hold a folded step ladder when it's not in use. Keep a stool or bench handy for hard-to-reach items. This one has a slot in the top for a handle to make it easy to carry as you clean. Pairs of pegs, left, support the vacuum hose and the mop. A nylon bag hung from a cup hook mounted on the wall holds all the vacuum-cleaner attachments as well as replacement vacuum bags; a whisk broom and feather duster also hang from cup hooks on the wall. Even the sides of the shelves are pressed into service, with cup hooks for a dusting brush and extension cord.

GROCERY-BAG DISPENSER

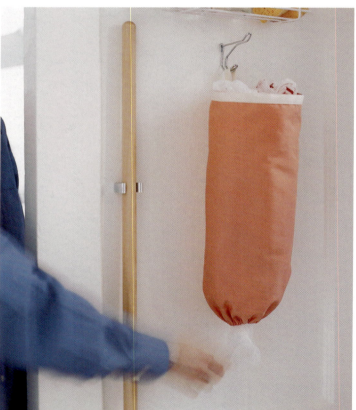

Instead of jamming plastic bags in a drawer, store them in this convenient tube. You will need a sixteen-by-twenty-inch piece of cotton twill fabric, three-quarter-inch-wide twill tape, and one-quarter-inch-wide elastic. Fold fabric in half lengthwise, right sides facing, and sew together a half inch from long edge, stopping three-quarters of an inch from the bottom; reinforce stitching at ends. Press seam open, including nonstitched section. Fold over bottom edge of tube, wrong sides facing, by three-quarters of an inch; stitch a half inch from fold. Fold over top of tube, right sides facing, by a half inch; press. Pin a twenty-inch length of twill tape to cover raw edge, aligning top with fold and one end with seam. Sew in place along top and bottom edges, stopping one and a half inches before seam at long end of tape. Cut a five-inch length of twill tape, and fold raw ends together; stitch them to twill tape at seam. Sew long end of tape over ends of loop, folding raw end under. Fasten a safety-pin to an eight-inch length of elastic, below; thread it through the tunnel at the bottom. Pull elastic through fabric until opening is two inches across; overlap ends of elastic and sew, then snip excess.

Chapter Eight

Fruit Wreath

STORAGE ROOMS

THE ATTIC, BASEMENT, AND GARAGE CAN BE THE ANSWERS TO ALL OF YOUR storage-related prayers. These rooms can fill quickly, though, and often do in a haphazard way; the key to keeping them working for you is deliberately arranging their contents. Have you forgotten what's in those two boxes? Can't get to a corner of the garage? Perhaps it's time for an overhaul. Go through your attic, basement, and garage with roomy garbage bags, and be brutally honest about what you'll really use in the future. Then, based on what's left, categorize and rearrange your things, mounting shelves and labeling possessions as you go. These rooms must be functional and safe—for you and your belongings—but they can be pretty as well.

ATTIC

BASEMENT

GARAGE

LONG-TERM STORAGE A streamlined attic storage area, opposite, can be built with components found at home-supply stores. The layout of the shelves leaves the window unobstructed, and the shelves are configured to accommodate special shapes, such as the long cylinders of wrapped carpets. A movable rack, left, is handy for hanging clothes, curtains, and other fabrics. Dry-clean out-of-season linens such as curtains, but don't keep them on the wire hangers provided by the dry cleaner because those will put creases in the fabric. Instead, cushion the bar of a cedar suit hanger with cotton hand towels, drape a single layer of acid-free tissue paper over it, then hang the fabric on that. To make a dust cover, cut a small opening in the end of a king-size, unbleached-cotton pillowcase, and reinforce the hole with a grommet. Pull the cover over the linens, passing the hanger through the grommet. From the hook, hang a sachet (cedar will help keep moths away) and a little bag to hold any hardware for the curtain. Linens that will be stored for more than a year should be refolded every so often to prevent any discoloration from occurring at the creases.

EASY IDENTIFICATION It can be easy to forget what clothes were packed in which box; one way to remember is to photograph the contents of each box or bag with a Polaroid camera, then tape it to the front. Attach photos to the containers with poly-vinyl acetate (PVA) adhesive, which won't attract insects. These archival boxes, free of acids and chemicals, are ideal for long-term storage. Wrap clothes in acid-free tissue before tucking them away.

MIRRORS AND ART Before storing a picture or a mirror, take a Polaroid of it to make an illustrated label. Then wrap it in acid-free tissue paper and sandwich the package between two layers of quarter-inch-thick foamboard, cut slightly larger than the frame. Secure the corners with foamboard strips and tape. Wrap in kraft paper, tie or tape closed, and tape photo to the front. Never store artwork flat; set wrapped items vertically on a shelf.

SUITCASE STORAGE Suitcases are great for storing clothes, jewelry, and fragile items; empty, they can themselves be stored inside one another. Because they are built for cargo holds, these leather, metal, plastic, and cloth cases offer some of the best protection around. Don't use cases that show any signs of mold or mildew, which can spread to objects kept within. Protect any objects you put inside with Bubble Wrap, cardboard, or another shock absorber so that they don't break when the suitcase is moved. Hatboxes, wastebaskets, and small metal garbage cans also work well for protecting breakables during storage.

RUGS AND CARPETS Among the simplest household items to store, rugs will stay fresh for years if they are treated well and kept in a dry place. First, clean the fabric. Cotton rugs can be machine-washed and line-dried if they aren't large and heavy. Smaller carpets can be hand-washed. But use professionals for a valuable handwoven carpet. They can usually wrap it for storage after it has been cleaned. If not, roll the rug tightly, wrap in kraft paper, and secure with paper tape and string. On the outside, write a description of the rug or tape a photo of it, noting its size.

CEDAR CLOSET This closet offers an added level of protection from pests. To be effective, all cedar closets must be nearly airtight and as dry as possible. A dehumidifier or a low-wattage bulb (fifteen watts for a small closet, twenty-five watts for a walk-in) flipped on from time to time will burn off excess humidity. Hanging bags should be made of fabric, which won't harm clothes the way plastics can. Be sure to pin labels to clothing bags so that you don't have to unzip each one to find the clothes you are searching for.

BASEMENT-PROOFING Basements pose two primary hazards for stored goods: moisture and dirt. Plumbing pipes, boilers, and hot-water heaters usually are in basements, so leaks and condensation are common. Oil and gas heating systems kick up a lot of dirt. Here, sports equipment and old tax files are kept in waterproof plastic storage bins. Compact boxes of tax records are kept on the top shelf because there is rarely a reason to look at them.

OFF THE FLOOR Adjustable two-by-sixes, set on a frame that rests on concrete blocks, elevate large items, such as seasonal furniture and even an upholstered chair. The blocks promote air circulation and protect the items from water and dampness. Hooks in the joists hold a chandelier and garden hoses. It's best to avoid hanging items from pipes, which can be damaged by the stress. Lightbulbs are encased in contractors' safety cages to keep them from shattering.

GROCERY SHELVES A well-kept basement invites regular use, and makes a good place to store extra groceries. Bulk-food storage near the stairway allows easy access, and the all-important flashlight sits in an obvious spot on a shelf. Unfinished wood shelving is an affordable way to keep everything you need handy, and you can tailor shelf heights to suit your needs. Martha devotes shelves to wine that is ready to drink and uses wooden crates to hold like items in one place. Whitewashed walls open up the space and fill it with more light.

WORK SPACE   Noisy projects won't disturb the rest of the house when the workshop is in the basement. Here, storage units hold tools, flammable and poisonous materials, and paints. A rubber mat can help prevent leg aches brought on by standing for long periods on bare concrete. A wall of Peg-Board above the work bench holds a shelf and provides visible storage for tools—they can be plucked off the wall and put away again with one hand.

DEHUMIDIFYING   It is essential to keep a basement dry and free of mildew; this electric dehumidifier is hung to drain directly into the sink, which means you don't need to remember to empty the pan. Its elevation lets the water drain straight down, so there's no need for a pump. A shelf attached to ceiling beams with chains provides stronger support than a wall shelf.

BOILER LINE   The clutter-free zone around a furnace, hot-water heater, or fuel tank should be at least eighteen inches deep. A yellow line painted on the floor serves as a reminder that the area around such equipment should remain free, especially of any kind of flammable material.

ONE-CAR GARAGE The ordinary one-car garage is usually a jumble of beach chairs and bikes, barbecue grills and gardening tools, wheelbarrows and skis. This revamped version reveals lots of untapped potential. Painting the bare wood white made a huge difference—the garage became a room. Pale green Peg-Board adds to the lightness of the space, and offers another advantage: Tools and objects are clearly silhouetted, making them easy to spot. A metal cart serves as a mobile work-bench, and the chair by the door provides a place to pull on gardening boots. A pan of sand on the floor catches oil drips from the car. The unfinished walls of a garage offer even more space to exploit: storage between the studs. Anything that can stand or lean, like a shovel, can be dropped in the "slots." With tall, light objects that might teeter over, like gardening stakes, just stretch a couple of bungee cords across the opening and hook them onto screws in the studs. The stakes stay tucked in their proper places and are easy to reach.

PARKING THE CAR Take the guesswork out of parking in the garage. Park the car, leaving ample space on all sides, then hang a ball on a string from the ceiling so it touches the windshield. When you park, drive in slowly until the ball taps your windshield.

WALL STORAGE Walls may be your only hope for storage in the garage because the car takes up most of the floor space. Bikes are hung on ladder hooks anchored to the studs. Flat items, such as folding chairs, make good use of space if hung behind a door; clipboards holding reminders about oil changes or plant watering are also hung where they will be sure to catch the eye.

PAINTBRUSH RACK Magnetic knife holders sold at kitchen-supply stores can be mounted to the wall with a few screws and will keep paintbrush bristles from being squashed. Hang the brushes bristle-end down for proper drying and to minimize the amount of dust that collects between the bristles. You can also store other metal tools and utensils this way.

Chances are slim you'll find room for a bona fide tool bench in a one-car garage. Instead, think compact and rolling—as in a metal cart from an industrial-supply catalog, fitted with Peg-Board on either side to hold the tools you most often use. The wheels allow you to roll the cart out into the driveway so you can work on a project outdoors. A plastic silverware tray in the cart's drawer, below, organizes small tools; a plastic cutting board becomes the work surface.

A hammer and nails are easy to find if everything is kept in its place. Create that place by marking the outlines of tools on a garage wall or above your workbench. We used black marker, but paint pens also work. The nuts and bolts can be organized in small clear-glass jars whose lids have been screwed to the underside of a shelf; use a hammer and nail to make holes in the lids before screwing them to the shelf.

WINDOW SHELVES The wall of shelving shown on pages 38 and 39 is actually three basic framed shelf units built off-site and fitted into the space with the addition of simple molding and trim. You can cut costs considerably if you have the bulk of the work produced at a wood shop instead of by an on-site carpenter. 1. Each unit is built to the measurements of the space; two of them fit between a wall and a window, and the third fits between the two windows. The basic cabinets for this project have a setback—the top shelves are shallower—providing a counter-like shelf at waist height with deeper shelves below it for storage. 2. Once the units are in place, a gap between cabinet and wall results above the baseboard. Installing a trim piece covers this gap and creates a built-in look. 3. Additional trim on the counter edge, cut to fit on-site, gives the units another furniture-like detail. 4. The window seats are actually wooden shelves, one and a quarter inches thick, that rest between the cabinets on wooden strip supports; an additional shelf runs below. 5. Holes drilled into the side of the bookcases hold pegs that make the shelves adjustable, a useful precaution for a built-in unit. 6. The cabinets are finished at the base with a board that runs the length of the unit; arched cutouts allow cleaning beneath and provide furniture-like feet that lighten the visual load of a wall-size unit.

USING A TEMPLATE

Many of the shelves shown in this book rest on brackets patterned after one of the templates on this page. Using a photocopier, you can reproduce and enlarge a template to create a paper or cardboard pattern for your own brackets (for a more slender, elegant bracket profile, elongate the curves or extend the bottom "tail"). Cut out the pattern and trace it onto wood; if the bracket shape has curves, use a jigsaw to cut it out. Brackets that will carry substantial weight, such as those under a bench, should be made with wood at least two inches thick. For most uses, however, one inch is an acceptable thickness.

MAKING A SHELF CLEAT

A cleat, bottom right, is the board that runs beneath a shelf and acts as a horizontal brace; it stabilizes the brackets and makes mounting the shelf on the wall easy. Because it distributes the load along the entire length of a shelf, the cleat also prevents sagging. To make a cleat, cut a board to the same length as the shelf. Mark the dimensions of the cleat's sawed end onto each bracket as a narrow rectangle at the top rear corner (shown as a crisscrossed rectangle in the template at top left). Cut out the rectangles to form notches that fit the cleat snugly. Attach the cleat to the brackets by inserting nails or screws through the back of the cleat. Then, after attaching the shelf to the top of the brackets and cleat, screw or nail the cleat to the wall.

FIVE BRACKET TEMPLATES

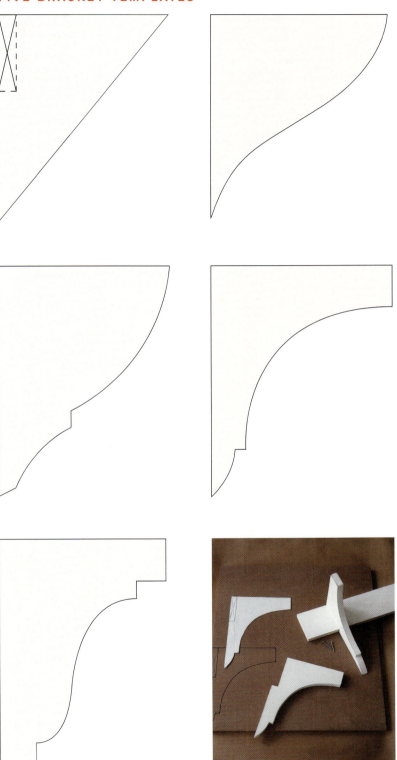

Items pictured but not listed may not be available or are from private collections. Addresses and telephone numbers of sources may change prior to or following publication, as may price and availability of any item.

COVER

Skylands **laundry baskets** (OLB001), $95 each; and painted **flower buckets** (GFB001, GFB002, and GFB003) in creamware, assorted sizes, $34 to $42 each; *from Martha by Mail,* 800-950-7130 or www.marthabymail.com. **Archival storage boxes,** assorted sizes and prices, *from Light Impressions,* 800-828-6216 or www.lightimpressionsdirect.com.

CHAPTER 1: KITCHEN

Page 14
Plastic-coated **wire shelving,** $4.15 to $4.75 per foot; and ⅜-inch-diameter **brass barrel fittings,** $3.99 per pair; *both from Gracious Home,* 1220 Third Avenue, New York, NY 10021; 212-517-6300 or 800-338-7809. **Curtain rod,** $3.35 per foot; and **brackets,** $3.95 per pair; *both from BZI Distributors,* 105 Eldridge Street, New York, NY 10002; 212-966-6690. Minimum purchase $25.

Page 15
Cypress wood **wall shelves,** built by *R. L. White & Son,* P.O. Box 8, Route 3, Hulls Cove, ME 04644; 207-288-5566. **Dishware,** from the Pil
livuyt Collection, *from Martha by Mail,* 800-950-7130 or www.marthabymail.com.

Page 16
Storage-box kit (#8212), $38.95, *from Light Impressions,* see above. **Storage cozies,** $20 to $40, *from Lillian Vernon,* 800-285-5555.

Page 17
Armoire, *from Ruby Beets Antiques,* 1703 Montauk Highway, Bridgehampton, NY

11932, or P.O. Box 596, Wainscott, NY 11975; 516-537-2802. Martha Stewart Everyday **paint** inside cabinet, "Potato Peel" (F14), *available at Kmart,* 800-866-0086 for stores.

Page 18
¼-inch-thick F-15 **felt** for drawer liners, *from Aetna Felt Corporation,* 2401 West Emmaus Avenue, Allentown, PA 18103; 610-791-0900. Minimum order 2 yards. **Tarnish-free cloth,** in drawer, $18.50 per yard, *by Eureka Manufacturing,* 47 Elm Street, Norton, MA 02766; 508-285-9881 or 800-376-8209.

Page 19
Borco vinyl **drafting board covering,** $7.81 to $8.80 per foot, *from NY Central Art Supply,* 62 Third Avenue, New York, NY 10003; 212-473-7705 or 800-950-6111.

Page 20
½-inch-diameter stainless-steel **tubing** (#8989K26), $18.33 for 6 feet, *from McMaster-Carr Supply Company,* www.mcmaster.com. Bygel **S hooks,** in chrome, $3.95 per pack of 10, *from Ikea,* 877-438-4532 or www.ikea.com.

Page 22
Countersink combination **drill bits,** *from Tool Crib of the North,* 800-884-9132 or tool crib.amazon.com; *also available at hardware stores nationwide.*

Page 23
Wooden peg **display rack** for platters (#925202), $13.95, *from Broadway Panhandler,* 477 Broome Street, New York, NY 10013; 212-966-3434. Rationell **pot lid holder,** $2.95, *from Ikea,* see above.

Page 24
½-inch-wide **cotton twill tape,** white, $1 for 2 yards, *from Daytona Trim,* 251 West 39th Street, New York, NY 10018; 212-354-1713.

Page 25
In-sink **colander** (#14-1057264), $29, *from Williams-Sonoma,* 800-541-2233 or www.williams-sonoma.com.

Page 26
Hooks (DHTY35S), 65¢ each, *from Gracious Home,* see above. Aluminum **cake pillar** (#425002), $27.95, *from Broadway Panhandler,* see above. **Cake platter,** $28, *from Dean and Deluca,* 560 Broadway, New York, NY 10012; 212-226-6800 or www.deananddeluca.com.

Pages 28 and 29
Armoire, *from Evergreen Antiques,* 1249 Third Avenue, New York, NY 10021; 212-744-5664. Antique **linen towels** for sack, *from Paula Rubenstein,* 65 Prince Street, New York, NY 10012; 212-966-8954. **Pine boxes** for drawers, *from Ikea,* see above. **Homasote** bulletin-board *from The Home Depot,* 800-430-3376 or www.homedepot.com; *or lumberyards nationwide.* Martha Stewart Everyday **paint,** "Homespun" (H03) on spice boxes; and "Beach Glass" (D24) on armoire shelves; *available at Kmart,* see above.

Page 30
Armoire, *from Monique Shay Antiques & Design,* 920 Main Street South, Woodbury, CT 06798; 203-263-3186. St. Charles **cabinet** with rollout shelves (now available in wood only), *from St. Charles of New York,* 150 East 58th Street, New York, NY 10155; 212-838-2812. Ball **mason jars,** from 75¢; and **spice jars,** from 75¢; *from Broadway Panhandler,* see above.

Page 33
Wall cabinet, *from The Home Depot,* see above. **Brass knobs** (#191), by Colonial Bronze, $6.23 each, *from Simon's Hardware & Bath,* 421 Third Avenue, New York, NY 10016; 212-532-9220 or 888-274-6667.

Page 34
Arches text-laid custom **sketchbook,** $45, *from NY Central Art Supply,* see above. Minimum purchase $15. Glassine **envelopes** (#151), $3.90 for pack of 25, *from American Printing and Envelope Company,* 800-221-9403. Wei T'O **deacidifying spray** (#11), $22; Gudy-O **archival tape,** $8.90, *from Talas,* 568 Broadway, New York, NY 10012; 212-219-0770 or www.talasonline.com.

CHAPTER 2: LIVING ROOMS

Page 36
Magazine holders, in "flax" (DMH001), $28 or $48 for set of 2, *from Martha by Mail,* 800-950-7130 or www.marthabymail.com.

Page 40
5-inch **acorn wood finial** (WF11), $6.25, *from Constantine's,* 800-223-8087 or www.constantines.com. 4-inch **mahogany finial** (F102-4), $21; 5-inch **mahogany finial** (F103-5M), $50; *from Boston Turning Works,* 120 Elm Street, Watertown, MA 02472; 617-924-4747 or www.bostonturningworks.com.

Page 46
1⅜-inch wood or metal **curtain finials,** $7 to $30 per pair, *from Bed Bath & Beyond,* 620 Sixth Avenue, New York, NY 10011; 212-255-3550 or 800-462-3966. **Bin pull handles:** brass or chrome, $9; polished or brushed nickel, $6; bronze, $6; cast iron, $4.95; *all from Restoration Hardware,* 935 Broadway, New York, NY 10010; 212-260-9479 or 800-762-1005 or www.restoration hardware.com. **Linen fabric,** $19.95 per yard, *from Rosen & Chadick,* 246 West 40th Street, New York, NY 10018; 212-869-0142 or www.rosenandchadick.com.

Page 47
8-by-10-inch **picture frames,** from $9.60, *from New York Central II,* 102 Third Avenue, New York, NY 10003; 212-420-6060.

Page 48
Blue fabric-covered **clamshell box,** from $117, *custom-made by Brewer & Cantelmo,* 350 Seventh Avenue, New York, NY 10001; 212-244-4600. **Raffia storage box with lid,**

$44; and **raffia storage box with drawer,** $75; *both from Zona,* 97 Greene Street, New York, NY 10012; 212-925-6750. **Slide-file master kit:** tan (#9586), $32.95; black (#9580), $37.95; *from Light Impressions,* 800-828-6216 or www.lightimpressionsdirect.com.

Page 49

Assorted men's **wool suiting fabric,** $21.95 to $100 per yard, *from B&J Fabrics,* 263 West 40th Street, New York, NY 10018; 212-354-8150. Jade polyvinyl acetate (PVA) **adhesive,** $7.80 for 16 ounces, *from NY Central Art Supply,* 62 Third Avenue, New York, NY 10003; 212-473-7705 or 800-950-6111.

Page 50

Acid-free or **Mylar sleeves** for LPs (M1258), package of 10, $13.40; 5 or more packages, $12.80 each; 10 or more packages, $11.80 each; *from Gaylord Bros.,* 800-448-6160.

Page 51

CD box, 5½-by-5⅞-by-5-inch (CDB554), $6.25 each for 3, $5.25 each for 10 to 19, $4.75 each for 20 or more; **Visi Case,** in clear (VCCD1), $3.25 each for 5, $2.65 each for 10 to 24, $2.25 each for 25 or more; **photo storage boxes** (RB13136), $11.95 each for 3, $10.95 each for 10 to 19, $9.45 each for 20 or more; **10-inch record-storage sleeves** (RSS10), $20.95 each for package of 25, $18.95 each for 3 to 14 packages, $16.45 each for 15 or more; and **12-inch sleeves** (RSS12), $22.95 for package of 25, $21.95 each for 2 to 14 packages, $17.95 each for 15 or more packages; *all from Gaylord Bros.,* see above. **Rubber stamps,** from $20, *from Klear Copy Design Rubber Stamps,* 104 West 27th Street, 5B, New York, NY 10001; 212-243-0357. Filmoplast archival cloth **book-repair tape,** 1¼-inch-wide, $12.45; 2-inch-wide, $15.60; 3¼-inch-wide, $24.95; *from Talas,* 568 Broadway, New York, NY 10012; 212-219-0770, or www.talasonline.com. **Straw box,** $4 to $33, *from Ad Hoc,* 136 Wooster, New York, NY 10012; 212-982-7703. **CD boxes,** from $19, *from Holdeverything,* 800-421-2264.

Page 52

Cabinet knobs by Colonial Bronze (#191), $6.23 each; and 12-inch **swivel mechanism** (#12C), $6.13; *from Simon's Hardware & Bath,* 421 Third Avenue, New York, NY 10016; 212-532-9220 or 888-274-6667.

CHAPTER 3: BEDROOM

Page 54

"Margo" **shoe-box files,** in "steel" (#170139-04), $14.95 each, *from Exposures,* 800-222-4947 or www.exposuresonline.com.

Page 58

Box-pleated **tablecloth,** *by D & F Workroom,* 150 West 25th Street, New York, NY 10001; 212-352-0160. **Nesting tables,** $4,500 for set of 4, *from Kentshire,* 37 East 12th Street, New York, NY 10003; 212-673-6644.

Pages 60 and 61

5-mm shelf **grommets** and spoon-shaped **supports,** *from Baer Supply Company,* 909 Forest Edge Drive, Vernon Hills, IL 60061; 800-944-2237. Borco vinyl **drafting board covering,** $7.81 to $8.80 per foot, *from NY Central Art Supply,* 62 Third Avenue, New York, NY 10003; 212-473-7705 or 800-950-6111. **Shirt, pant rod,** and **skirt clip hangers** and hooks, *from Gracious Home,* 1220 Third Avenue, New York, NY 10021; 212-517-6300 or 800-338-7809. **Quilted hanger,** $15 for 4, *from Holdeverything,* 800-421-2264. **Leather boxes,** $165 to $240, *from Galileo,* 37 Seventh Avenue, New York, NY 10011; 212-243-1629.

Page 62

Bunny receiving blanket, $11.99 for 5; **rickrack receiving blanket,** $11.99 for 5; and hooded embroidered yellow **duck towel,** $14.99; from the Martha Stewart Everyday Baby Baby collection, *at Kmart,* 800-866-0086 for stores. **Trouser rack** (#57-2192235), $40; and unpainted maple **accessory boxes,** *from Holdeverything,* see above. Pink **drawer pulls,** $21 each, *from Restoration Hardware,* 935 Broadway, New York, NY 10010; 212-260-9479 or 800-762-1005 or www.restoration hardware.com. White cotton piqué fabric **shelf lining,** $11.95 per yard, *from Rosen & Chadick,* 246 West 40th Street, New York, NY 10018; 212-869-0142 or www.rosenand chadick.com. ¾-inch nickel-finish **cup hooks,** 65¢, *from Gracious Home,* see above.

Page 63

Stepladder, $57.99 to $89.99, *from Gracious Home,* see above. Emu **metal boxes,** $6.95, *from Ikea,* 877-438-4532 or www.ikea.com. Gray **archival boxes,** *from Talas,* 568 Broadway, New York, NY 10012; 212-219-0770 or www.talasonline.com.

Page 64

Hangers, *from Holdeverything,* see above.

Page 66

Rubberex 1⅝-inch **plate caster,** $5.62 each, *from Simon's Hardware & Bath,* 421 Third Avenue, New York, NY 10016; 212-532-9220 or 888-274-6667. ½-inch **decorative tack** (#682), *from C. S. Osborne & Co.,* 125 Jersey Street, Harrison, NJ 07029; 973-483-3232. **Knobs,** $7 to $12, *from Olde Good Things,* 124 West 24th Street, New York, NY 10011; 212-989-8401. Cedar-fresh **drawer liners,** *from Gracious Home,* see above. **Sweater box,** $20; and **sock boxes,** $12 each; *from Holdeverything,* see above. **Acid-free paper,** $1.50 per sheet, *from Talas,* see above.

CHAPTER 4: BATHROOM

Page 70

Brushed-aluminum **lotion bottle,** $5.75; **mister bottle,** $3.50; and **tall bottle,** $5.50; *all from Mxyplyzyk,* 125 Greenwich Avenue, New York, NY 10014; 212-989-4300. **Flat-backed storage cups,** *from Bed Bath & Beyond,* 620 Sixth Avenue, New York, NY 10011; 212-255-3550 or 800-462-3966.

Page 71

Lombok basket, $45, *from Be Seated,* 66 Greenwich Avenue, New York, NY 10011; 212-924-8444. Custom-made **cubbyhole shelves,** *by Christopher M. Cavallaro,* 212-475-4371. Glass **dressing jars,** $8.50 to $17.50 each, depending on size; 7-ounce **metal cup,** $8.50; and glass **applicator jar,** $11; *all from Arista Surgical Supply,* 67 Lexington Avenue, New York, NY 10010; 212-679-3694. Minimum mail order $25.

Page 72

Stainless-steel box, $22.95, *from Mxyplyzyk,* see above.

Page 74

Linen/rayon curtain fabric, $21.95 per yard, *from B&J Fabrics,* 263 West 40th Street, New York, NY 10018; 212-354-8150.

Page 76

Fieldcrest Royal Velvet **towels:** washcloth, $4.99; hand towel, $8.99; and bath towel, $11.99; *all from Bloomingdale's,* 800-555-7467 for stores. **Linen huck towels,** *from Ulster Linen Company,* 148 Madison Avenue, New York, NY 10016; 212-684-5534 or www.ulsterlinen.com. *To the trade only.* **Drawer pulls,** *from Garber Hardware,* 49 Eighth Avenue, New York, NY 10014; 212-929-3030.

Page 77

Custom embroidery, *by Penn & Fletcher,* 21-07 41st Avenue, 5th Floor, Long Island City, NY 11101; 212-239-6868 or www.penn andfletcher.com.

CHAPTER 5: HOME OFFICE

Page 83

Bone folder (CFT009), $5, *from Martha by Mail,* 800-950-7130 or www.marthabymail. com. 16-by-20-inch Windberg multimedia **art panel,** and yellow and gray **paper,** *from NY Central Art Supply,* 62 Third Avenue, New York, NY 10003; 212-473-7705 or 800-950-6111. **Yellow elastic** (art #4656), *from Mokuba,* 55 West 39th Street, New York, NY 10018; 212-869-8900.

Page 84

Homasote bulletin-board material *from The Home Depot,* 800-430-3376 or www.home depot.com or *lumberyards nationwide.*

Page 85

Assorted **file boxes,** *from Ikea,* 877-438-4532 or www.ikea.com.

Page 86

Linen canvas, *from NY Central Art Supply,* see above; *also available at Pearl Paint,* 308 Canal Street, New York, NY 10013; 212-431-7932 or 800-221-6845. **Tacks,** $7.95

for 100, *from BZI Distributors,* 105 Eldridge Street, New York, NY 10002; 212-966-6690. Minimum purchase $25.

Page 87
Nineteenth century Hungarian **Armoire**, *from Evergreen Antiques,* 1249 Third Avenue, New York, NY 10021; 212-744-5664.

Page 88
Cube Mate **storage compartments**, *from Sam Flax,* 12 West 20th Street, New York, NY 10011; 212-620-3038.

Page 89
"Islander" white enamel-top **table**, $1,080, *from Rhubarb Home,* 26 Bond Street, New York, NY 10012; 212-533-1817. "Eiffel" metal shelf **brackets**, $14 each for small, *from Anthropologie,* 375 West Broadway, New York, NY 10012; 212-343-7070.

Page 90
Fire-resistant extra-deep **file** by Sentry, $127.60, *from Value-Tique Inc.,* 800-444-2135.

Page 91
Organizers, *from Holdeverything,* 800-421-2264. **Document boxes**, from $7.95, *from Light Impressions,* 800-828-6216 or www.light impressionsdirect.com. Print **envelope box**, $7.20, *from Gaylord Bros.,* 800-448-6160. **Stationery box**, *from Kate's Paperie,* 561 Broadway, New York, NY 10012; 212-941-9816.

Page 92
Moppe wooden **mini-chest**, from $14.95, *from Ikea,* see above. **Ribbon box**, $68, *from Papivore,* 117 Perry Street, New York, NY 10014; 212-627-6055.

Pages 93 to 95
Homasote bulletin-board material, *from The Home Depot,* 800-430-3376 or www.home depot.com or *lumberyards nationwide.*

CHAPTER 6: WORKROOMS
Page 99
Dowels, brackets, and shelving **hardware**, *from The Home Depot,* 800-430-3376 or www.homedepot.com. **Storage boxes**, *from Ikea,* 877-438-4532 or www.ikea.com.

Page 102
Terra-cotta **pots**, *from The Grass Roots Garden,* 131 Spring Street, New York, NY 10012; 212-226-2662. Natural Belgian **linen**, $20 to $70 per yard, *from Pearl Paint,* 308 Canal Street, New York, NY 10013; 212-431-7932 or 800-221-6845. Martha Stewart Everyday Garden steady-grip jersey **gloves**, $3.49, *from Kmart,* 800-866-0086 for stores.

Page 103
Painted **flower buckets:** small (GFB001), $34; medium (GFB002), $38; and large (GFB003), $42, *from Martha by Mail,* 800-950-7130 or www.marthabymail.com. Rubber **boots** (#3005), $62, and galvanized **stool** (#465211), $155, *from Smith & Hawken,* 800-776-3336 or www.smithandhawken.com.

Page 104
Ball-point **hooks**, 50¢ to $1, *from Simon's Hardware & Bath,* 421 Third Avenue, New York, NY 10016; 212-532-9220 or 888-274-6667. **Storage boxes**, *from Ikea,* see above.

Page 105
Barrel fittings, *from Gracious Home,* 1220 Third Avenue, New York, NY 10021; 212-517-6300 or 800-338-7809. **Bamboo rods** (#03-162), $14.95 for 12; and **plant markers** (#14-310); $10.95 for 25; *from Gardener's Supply Co.,* 800-863-1700 or www.gardeners.com.

CHAPTER 7: UTILITY ROOMS
Page 108
Apothecary jar (OCA003), $82, *from Martha by Mail,* 800-950-7130 or www.marthabymail.com.

Page 110
Binder rings: 1-inch, $2.75 per 12 pack; 1½-inch, $1.19 per 3 pack; and 2-inch, $1.99 per 5-pack; *from Staples Direct,* 800-333-3330. **Metal shelves** by InterMetro, $310, *from New York Store Fixture Company,* 167 Bowery, New York, NY 10002; 212-226-0044 or 800-336-8353 (outside New York only). Wooden **drawer organizers**, $15 to $25; and canvas **laundry sorter**, $199; *from Holdeverything,* 800-421-2264. Fold-down **shelf brackets:** 8-inch, $19.60 each; 12-inch, $21.94 each; and 16-inch, $36.73 each; *from Simon's Hardware & Bath,* 421 Third Avenue, New York, NY 10016; 212-532-9220 or 888-274-6667.

Page 111
Assorted plastic **containers**, priced up to $11.99, *from The Container Store,* 800-733-3532 or www.containerstore.com.

Pages 112 and 113
Brass card holders, $2 each, *from Simon's Hardware & Bath,* see above. **Acid-free tissue paper**, $50.75 for 500 sheets, *from NY Central Art Supply,* 62 Third Avenue, New York, NY 10003; 212-473-7705 or 800-950-6111. **Clear cellophane**, $11 per 100-foot roll, *from New York Cake & Baking Distributor,* 56 West 22nd Street, New York, NY 10010; 212-675-2253.

Pages 116 and 117
Runner (NFP27), $5.99 per foot, *from Ed Herrington Inc.,* 312 White Hill Lane, Hillsdale, NY 12529; 518-325-3131. **Roller shades**, *from East End Installations,* 800-287-4554.

Page 118
Shaker pegs: 30¢ each for 3½-inch (#98T11); and 15¢ for 1¾-inch (#98T10); *from Constantine's,* 800-223-8087 or www.constantines.com.

Page 119
Debatt wine rack (#46103009), $6.95, *from Ikea,* 877-438-4532 or www.ikea.com.

Page 120
Custom-made **crock lids**, *from Klatt Sheet Metal,* P.O. Box 156, South Jamesport, NY 11970; 631-722-3515.

Page 121
Flat-top **waste bin**, in Martha's Green (HTB003), $63, *from Martha by Mail,* 800-950-7130 or www.marthabymail.com. Pavo **key cabinet**, $4.95, *from Ikea,* see above. **Homasote** bulletin-board material *from The Home Depot,* 800-430-3376 or www.home depot.com or *lumberyards nationwide.*

CHAPTER 8: STORAGE ROOMS
Page 124
Archival **storage boxes**, assorted sizes and prices, *from Light Impressions,* 800-828-6216 or www.lightimpressionsdirect.com.

Page 126
Garment rack (#93-365510), $129, *from Holdeverything,* 800-421-2264. **Archival boxes**, $4.15 to $50, *from Talas,* 568 Broadway, New York, NY 10012; 212-219-0770 or www.talasonline.com.

Page 127
Industrial steel **shelving**, *from Karp Associates,* 54-54 43rd Street, Maspeth, NY 11378; 718-784-2105. Minimum order $25. See-through **storage box** (GH744170), $1.55 each (12 per carton, minimum purchase 1 carton); **container with white lid** (GH744171), $3.50 each (12 per carton, minimum purchase 1 carton); **gray storage container with detachable lid** (GN422608), $7.30 per box, $3.55 per lid; and **gray storage container with detachable lid** (GN422606), $8.50 per box, $3.55 per lid; *all from Global Industrial Equipment,* 22 Harbor Park Drive, Port Washington, NY 11050; 516-625-8787 or 800-645-1232 or www.globalindustrial.com. Free catalog.

Page 130
Steel **shelving**, and gray plastic **storage bins**, *from Global Industrial Equipment,* see above. **Rubbermaid storage bins**, *from Kmart,* 800-866-0086 for stores. **Cardboard storage boxes**, *from Staples Direct,* 800-333-3330. Sten **shelving**, pictured at bottom, *from Ikea,* 877-438-4532 or www.ikea.com.

Page 131
Workbench, rolling tool cart, and **storage unit**, *from Global Industrial Equipment,* see above. **Peg-Board**, and **shelving**, *from Pergament Home Center,* 825 Montauk Highway, East Patchogue, NY 11772; 516-447-6200.

Page 134
18-inch-long magnetic **knife holder**, $16.95, *from Broadway Panhandler,* 477 Broome Street, New York, NY 10013; 212-966-3434.

Page 135
Cart (SCH236), $95.35; and **drawer** (SCD13), $21.50; *from Turnkey,* 800-828-7540. Unfinished **Peg-Board**, $6.25 per foot, *from Shaker Workshops,* P.O. Box 8001, Ashburnham, MA 01430; 800-840-9121. Free catalog.

CONTRIBUTORS

Special thanks to all those whose insight and dedication contributed to the creation of this volume, notably: Stephen Antonson, Roger Astudillo, Celia Barbour, Jesse Foley Brink, Kerin Brooks, Amy Conway, Barbara de Wilde, Stephen Drucker, James Dunlinson, Stephen Earle, Jamie Fedida, Stephanie Garcia, Matthew Gleason, Angela Gubler, Eric Hutton, Brennan Travis Kearney, Peter Mars, Jim McKeever, Hannah Milman, Melissa Morgan, Janine Nichols, Eric A. Pike, George Planding, Debra Puchalla, Shax Riegler, Paul Robinson, Nikki Rooker, Scot Schy, Curtis Smith, Ellen Tarlin, Lindsey Taylor, Gael Towey, Alison Vanek, and Bunny Wong. Thanks also to Oxmoor House, Clarkson Potter, Satellite Graphic Arts, and R. R. Donnelley and Sons. And thank you to Martha for inspiring us to reach for the best.

PHOTOGRAPHY

WILLIAM ABRANOWICZ
cover, 2–3, 8, 47, 84, 85, 88, 138

ANTHONY AMOS
16 *(top)*, 105 *(bottom left)*, 126 *(top left)*, 127, 128, 132–33, 134 *(all but far right)*, 135 *(top right and far left)*

CHUCK BAKER
14 *(top left)*, 15

JONN COOLIDGE
56, 57, 58 *(top left and bottom right)*, 59

SUSIE CUSHNER
134 *(far right)*

CARLTON DAVIS
48

REED DAVIS
22 *(top)*, 86 *(bottom left and bottom right)*, 91 *(all but bottom left)*, 120 *(bottom)*, 121 *(bottom)*, 122 *(bottom left and right)*, 130, 131

TODD EBERLE
18 *(top right)*, 45

FORMULA z/s
20, 22 *(bottom)*, 23, 82, 83

DANA GALLAGHER
32, 76 *(bottom left and bottom right)*, 104

GENTL & HYERS
66 *(top left)*, 67, 71 *(bottom)*, 72 *(top left)*, 76 *(top left and top right)*, 89, 100 *(top left)*

MATTHEW HRANEK
110, 111 *(top)*

GRACE HUANG
49, 90, 91 *(bottom left)*, 92 *(bottom)*, 93

LISA HUBBARD
24 *(top)*, 25, 26, 27 *(top)*, 70 *(top left and bottom)*, 71 *(top)*, 72 *(center and bottom)*

THIBAULT JEANSON
38–39, 136

KIT LATHAM
4, 102 *(top left)*, 103

STEPHEN LEWIS
44, 46 *(top right)*, 50, 51, 63, 70 *(top right)*, 95, 102 *(far right)*, 121 *(far right)*

MINH + WASS
62

VICTORIA PEARSON
108, 109

DAVID PRINCE
31, 35 *(top)*, 77 *(top)*, 100 *(top right)*, 120 *(top)*

JASON SCHMIDT
5, 33, 42, 52, 53, 58 *(top right)*, 74 *(bottom)*, 116, 117, 118, 119, 122 *(top)*, 123, 137

VICTOR SCHRAGER
135 *(bottom)*

GEORGE SEPER
30

ROBERT TARDIO
64, 65

LUCA TROVATO
19 *(bottom)*, 27 *(bottom)*, 60, 61, 66 *(bottom left and center)*, 111 *(bottom)*, 112, 113, 114, 115, 126 *(bottom)*, 129

SIMON WATSON
14 *(all but top left)*, 16 *(all but top)*, 17, 19 *(top and right)*, 28, 29, 40 *(top right)*, 41, 46 *(all but top right)*, 86 *(top left)*, 87, 94, 98, 99

WENDELL T. WEBBER
40 *(top left and bottom)*, 100 *(bottom right)*, 121 *(top)*

ANNA WILLIAMS
endpapers, book plate, 6–7, 10–11, 12, 24 *(bottom right)*, 34, 35 *(bottom left and right)*, 36, 43, 54, 68, 77 *(all but top)*, 78–79, 80, 92 *(top and far right)*, 96, 101, 102 *(center)*, 105 *(top right)*, 106, 124

BRUCE WOLF
18 *(far left and bottom right)*, 21, 73, 74 *(top left)*, 75

INDEX